MW00985131

A GIFT FOR:

_____

FROM:

_____

PEOPLE
in the BIBLE

ENCOUNTER 125

HEROES, VILLAINS &

'ORDINARY' SOULS

DR. WOODROW KROLL

FROM RADIO'S *Back to the Bible* BROADCAST

Nashville, Tennessee

Show yourself an example

of those who believe.

1 TIMOTHY 4:12

*Trust in Him
at all times, O people.*

Psalm 62:8

FOREWORD

Some of my earliest childhood memories are sitting in Sunday school listening to Bible stories. Gifted men and women used flashcards, flannelgraph, and object lessons to make the men and the women of the Bible come alive. Each Bible character made a deep impression on my heart and taught me how to or how not to live.

Today, I am still fascinated with the "who's who" in the Word of God. The Bible is a collection of candid snapshots, a photo album of unvarnished proofs. Hundreds of people—good, bad, and "normal"—were caught in the unblinking lens of Scripture. Only one perfect man appears, and His picture is on every page of the book. But many saints, despite problems and imperfections, chose to trust and obey God. Others glowered into the camera, frowning, fuming, leaving behind an ugly picture of shame and selfishness.

Life stories from the pages of Scripture contain important lessons to be learned. And what a contrast in faith, character, and obedience:

These are just a few stories listed in God's Word. The list could go on, recounting the countless men and women who are remembered for how they lived. And there are important life-lessons we should take away from each biography.

Dr. Woodrow Kroll has done an outstanding and exhaustive search of the *People in the Bible,* skillfully telling their stories in quick snapshots. This "everything you ever wanted to know about" Bible characters study not only gives you the Scripture reference, identification, and story line of each person, but Woodrow leaves you with a spiritual application from the life of each famous or infamous case study.

All of the men and women found in this book have left us a legacy. As the apostle Paul wrote in Romans 14:7, *"None of us lives to himself, and no one dies to himself."* What story will your life tell? What legacy will it leave?

May Dr. Woodrow Kroll's *People of the Bible* help you mold and shape the story you leave behind.

DR. DAVID JEREMIAH

INTRODUCTION

Everybody has a story. The Bible is filled with people great and small, and each one of them has a story. God loves to tell their stories because God loves people. We're not faceless blobs to Him; we're unique, precious, treasured. No matter how ordinary we see ourselves, God sees us each as extraordinary. God knows your name. He knows your story. He even knows the hair count on your head.

The whole Bible is a record of the soap-opera relationships between God and people. He's one-hundred-percent loving and trustworthy, while people are consistently fickle, foolish, and even downright mean. But God still loves us and takes us back whenever we repent and seek His forgiveness.

As you encounter each of the Bible people in this book, keep in mind that these are real people with real-life stories. They're not fictional characters; they're people just like you and me. Each person has a lesson to teach us about life. In every circumstance, you can choose either to live for God or to live for yourself, and these Bible people have much to teach about the consequences of our choices.

Some of the unique people in the Bible are well known to us—people like David, Abraham, Paul, Sarah and Ruth. Others are, admittedly, rather obscure—people like Ebed-melech, Mephibosheth, Jashobeam and Barzillai. Never mind. Their stories are just as intriguing and interesting as those better known to us.

So from A to Z, get ready to meet 125 of the thousands of heroes, villains, and "ordinary" people in the Bible. Get to know the God these people encountered by getting to know the people and their stories. After all, everybody has a story.

We have so great
a cloud of
witnesses
surrounding us.

HEBREWS 12:1

AARON

When Things Get Out of Control

Carolyn was a leader in her Bible study group. But one night on a date, she allowed things to get out of hand. Her passion got the best of her and she sinned. Her purity was lost and her self-esteem shattered. She sought forgiveness and received it, but Carolyn's

NAME: "Exalted" or "High Mountain"
DATE: 15th Century BC
IDENTIFICATION: brother of Moses; high priest of Israel
STORY LINE: God's professional failed to keep Israel from sinning
READ IT IN THE BIBLE: Exodus 32:1–29

baby was a constant reminder that a loss of control even for a moment can change your life forever.

Aaron knew that feeling, too. He was Moses' older brother and was designated by God as Moses' official spokesman. Aaron was 83 when the brothers challenged Pharaoh. He accompanied Moses partway up the holy mountain and saw the vision of God.

Moses consecrated Aaron as the first high priest of Israel. The Tabernacle was under his supervision. To the Hebrew people, Aaron was second only to Moses in importance.

But while Moses was with God on the mountaintop, in a moment of weakness Aaron gave in to the people's demands for an idol to worship. He melted down their jewelry and made a golden image of a calf. The people got drunk and began to engage in a sexual orgy around the idol. God decided to destroy the people, but Moses interceded for them and they were spared, no thanks to Aaron.

For the Christian, self–control is really Spirit–control. When we yield ourselves and our bodies to the Holy Spirit, He uses us for God's glory. When we maintain our own control, that's when things get out of hand. Ask the Holy Spirit to help you control your thoughts, emotions, and actions. Don't become a spiritual casualty because you let things get out of hand.

ABIGAIL

An Unhappy Marriage

Sometimes you can see it coming. You warn them, but they don't listen. That's what happened to Jasmine. She married the wrong man. Her husband did not abuse her, but he often was drunk and surly. When

NAME: "Father of Joy"
DATE: 10th Century BC
IDENTIFICATION: Wife of Nabal who later became the wife of David
STORY LINE: Abigail's wisdom saved her foolish husband's life
READ IT IN THE BIBLE: 1 Samuel 25:1–44

Jasmine trusted Christ, however, she decided to make the best of a bad marriage.

She was encouraged by the story of Abigail in the Old Testament. Abigail was the wife of Nabal, and like Jasmine's husband, he was no prize. Although he was a wealthy sheep owner, Nabal was ill–tempered and drank heavily.

David and his men protected Nabal's property,

but when they requested some supplies in return, Nabal brusquely refused. Infuriated, David took four hundred men to kill Nabal and would have done so had it not been for Abigail. A wise woman, she assembled some supplies and took them to David. She apologized for her foolish husband's behavior. David thanked God for using Abigail to keep him from his own foolish plans of revenge.

Are you in an unpleasant marriage like Jasmine or Abigail? There's hope for you, too, if you respond in wisdom. First Corinthians 7 outlines God's plan for responding to an unbelieving spouse. It doesn't include divorce, but something better—wisdom. Live in such a way that your godly character will bring conviction to your husband or wife, and maybe even salvation.

So angry was Nabal at Abigail's actions that ten days later he suffered a stroke and died. David rewarded Abigail by marrying her himself. There's no guarantee your story will turn out the same way, but you can demonstrate the same wisdom. Ask God for help. Ask Him to change your husband or wife. Ask Him to change you.

ABRAHAM

Being a Person of Faith

James Kraft sold his cheese products out of the back of a horse–drawn wagon, but he wasn't doing well. Then he determined to let God become his business partner, and Kraft Cheese was built into a multibillion–dollar business. The difference was faith.

NAME: "Father of a Multitude"
DATE: 22nd Century BC
IDENTIFICATION: The friend of God and first great patriarch of Israel
STORY LINE: Abraham proved himself to be a man of great faith
READ IT IN THE BIBLE: Genesis 11:27–12:9; 22:1–14

The original man of faith was Abraham, the first great patriarch of Israel. God called him to leave everything he was familiar with in Ur of the Chaldees and go to a strange land. Abraham is the primary model of faithfulness both in Judaism and Christianity.

Abraham's life was characterized by trusting God, but nowhere was his faith more severely tested than at

Mt. Moriah. When Abraham was 75, God promised him a son, but Isaac was not born until Abraham was 100 (Genesis 21:5). Abraham not only had faith, he had patience. But when God asked him to sacrifice the son he had so patiently awaited, it didn't make sense. Nevertheless, the next morning Isaac and he left on the three-day journey to Mt. Moriah.

Abraham didn't understand what God was doing, but he trusted the character of God. Faith doesn't always need understanding; if it did, it wouldn't be faith. But God always takes notice of believing faith. He rewarded Abraham by providing a substitute sacrifice for Isaac. Abraham's greatest test of faith was passed.

Your tests of faith may not be as dramatic as this, but they could be just as non-understandable. Ralph Waldo Emerson said, "All I have seen teaches me to trust God for all I have not seen." Today, identify some area of your life where trusting God is essential, even if it makes no sense. Then, become a model of faith.

ACHAN

You Cannot Successfully Hide Sin

Martha Stewart was America's homemaker. But when she secretly dumped her ImClone stock and tried to hide the transaction, she was caught and convicted. Her previous successes couldn't hide her guilt.

Israel was successful too. They had just destroyed the nearly impregnable outpost of Jericho. There were high–fives all around. Then came Ai.

NAME: "Trouble"

DATE: 15th Century BC

IDENTIFICATION: Son of Carmi of the tribe of Judah in Joshua's day

STORY LINE: Achan caused Israel's defeat at Ai due to his dishonesty

READ IT IN THE BIBLE: Joshua 6:1–7:26

Ai was a much smaller, less strategic city than the great fortress of Jericho. Still, when Joshua sent his troops against it, Israel was soundly defeated because of the sin of one man—Achan.

God specifically had told Israel not to confiscate

any of the spoils of war from Jericho, but Achan disobeyed. When confronted by Joshua, Achan admitted, "When I saw among the spoils a beautiful Babylonian garment, two hundred shekels of silver, and a wedge of gold weighing fifty shekels, I coveted them and took them" (Joshua 7:21). He unsuccessfully hid them under his tent.

Achan joined the parade of people who have failed to successfully hide their sin from God. When Adam and Eve disobeyed God they attempted to hide from Him in the Garden of Eden; they failed. When Moses killed an Egyptian, he attempted to hide the man's body in the sand; he failed. Achan tried to hide his sin under his tent; he failed too.

The warning of Proverbs 28:13 is unambiguous: "He who covers his sins will not prosper, but whoever confesses and forsakes them will have mercy." If you have something you're trying to hide from God today, apply the 1 John 1:9 principle to your life. Cleansing is always better than hiding, and far more successful. Come clean before God.

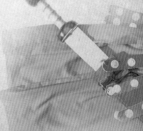

ADAM
Keeping It Together

Michael Jackson had every advantage. He was famous, wealthy, the king of pop. But his peculiarities led to his being charged with seven counts of performing

Name: "Earth" or "To be Red"
Date: Unknown; pre–4000 BC
Identification: The first man, created by God on the sixth day
Story Line: Even a perfect environment couldn't prevent sin
Read it in the Bible: Genesis 1:1–3:24; Romans 5:12–21

lewd or lascivious acts on a child under 14. Michael had it all, but he couldn't keep it together.

The first man in history had more advantages than anybody. Adam was created in the image of God. God placed him in a perfect environment with beautiful trees and fragrant flowers. And when Adam was lonely, God made a lovely woman just for him. Adam had everything. His gene pool was perfect; his environment was superlative. But it wasn't enough.

Adam couldn't keep it together.

Why do athletes and movie stars self-destruct? The same reason we do—sin. Adam had the opportunity to do good or evil; sadly he exercised his option to sin. As a result, our first parents became sinful, and two sinful parents will produce a sinful child every time (Job 14:4).

Because Adam sinned, he died in every sense of the word—physically, spiritually, emotionally. As his descendants, that death is passed on to all of us. But there's another Adam, the Last Adam, named Jesus Christ (1 Corinthians 15:45). What the first Adam lost for us through disobedience in the garden, the Last Adam gained back through obedience at a place called Calvary.

If you're having trouble keeping it all together today, let Christ Jesus get it together for you. He died to save you from your sin. Do what the Bible says: "Believe on the Lord Jesus Christ and you will be saved" (Acts 16:31). Jesus will keep it together for you.

AMOS

God's 'Little People'

William Carey was an apprentice shoemaker at age 14. He came to Christ as Savior at age 18. Later when a high society Englishman wanted to embarrass Mr. Carey he said, "I hear, Mr. Carey, that you were a cobbler."

NAME: "Carry" or "Bear a Burden"
DATE: 8th Century BC
IDENTIFICATION: Shepherd from Tekoa, called by God as a prophet
STORY LINE: Amos denounced the corruption of Northern Kingdom
READ IT IN THE BIBLE: Amos 1:1–2; 6:1–14; 8:1–1

"Oh, no, my lord, not a cobbler," replied the humble Carey, "just a shoemaker."

Carey's motto was, "Expect great things from God. Attempt great things for God." He was one of God's "little people" who went to India and, along with two friends, attempted great things for God. Together they founded 26 churches and 126 schools with a total enrollment of ten thousand. They translated the Bible into 44 languages and produced grammars and dictionaries. Carey and friends organized India's first medical mission, savings bank, seminary, Indian girls' school, and Bengali newspaper. Their accomplishments were astounding, especially for such humble beginnings.

The prophet Amos also was one of God's "little people." He had humble beginnings, too. He was but a shepherd living in Tekoa, an unassuming village about ten miles south of Jerusalem. But God does not look on our humble beginnings when He chooses someone to attempt great things for him. God spoke to Amos in a vision, and the shepherd–turned–prophet mightily denounced the idol worship, graft, and corruption of Israel. He was just a herdsman and a tender of sycamore fruit (Amos 7:14), but Amos spoke effectively with the highest authority possible—the authority of God.

It doesn't matter who you are; what matters is what God wants to do through you. If you feel like one of the "little people" in the church, be encouraged. Our big God likes to use little people to impact the world.

ANDREW

Living in Tall Shadows

You have to feel sorry for Johann Christian Bach. Not only was he a lesser light than his older brother Carl Philipp Emanuel Bach, he was the son of the great Johann Sebastian Bach. It's not easy living in the tall shadows of another person, especially a relative.

NAME: "Manly" or "A Strong Man"
DATE: 1st Century AD
IDENTIFICATION: Brother of Peter, mentioned 12 times in the Bible
STORY LINE: Andrew lived in his brother's shadow all his life
READ IT IN THE BIBLE: John 1:19–42

Esau lived in Jacob's shadow. Aaron lived in Moses' shadow. And Andrew lived in Peter's shadow.

Andrew is mentioned twelve times in the New Testament, half of those times simply as "Simon Peter's brother." People identified him as, "Andrew, you know, Peter's brother."

Andrew never allowed that to get to him. He was a disciple of John the Baptist, but when John identified Jesus as the Lamb of God, Andrew immediately followed Jesus. His first act as a Christ–follower was to find his brother, announce to him they had found the Messiah, and bring Peter to Jesus. Andrew is the premier example of being a faithful witness to our families.

Tradition says that Andrew was martyred at Patrae in Achaia by crucifixion on an X–shaped cross. According to Eusebius, Andrew's field of labor was Scythia, the region north of the Black Sea. For this reason, he became the patron saint both of Russia and of Scotland.

You may not be a "Peter," but could you be an "Andrew"? Peter got more press, but Andrew got Peter. Maybe Peter caught more fish, but Andrew caught a bigger fish. Even if you live in the shadow of a more famous sibling, be yourself. Faithfully do what God has given you to do. Who knows? You may just catch a bigger fish than anyone.

ANNA

Senior 'Saints'

The Bible praises those who have entered the senior phase of life. First Peter 5:5 says younger people are to submit respectfully to their elders. Solomon says gray hair is "the splendor of old men" (Proverbs 20:29). But right living is not the automatic consequence of

NAME: "Favor" or "Gracious"

DATE: 1st Century AD

IDENTIFICATION: Daughter of Phanuel; a prophetess in Jerusalem

STORY LINE: Anna ministered in the Temple while awaiting the Messiah

READ IT IN THE BIBLE: Luke 2:21–40

growing older. The same verse that says "the silver–haired head is a crown of glory" cautions, "if it is found in the way of righteousness" (Proverbs 16:31).

Anna was a senior who decided to be active and live rightly. No rocking chair for her. She had only been married seven years when her husband died. She remained a widow the rest of her life and now was

84 years old. She could have been bitter at the hardship of her life and now her advanced age, but she refused. Instead, she worshiped God every day in the Temple the only way she could, with prayer and fasting.

When Jesus' parents came to the Temple to present Him to the Lord, Anna approached them and spoke of the baby to all who were looking for the redemption of Jerusalem. Anna was old, but age was no deterrent to ministry.

Anna earned the praise of Luke as he wrote his gospel, but not because she was old. Age doesn't automatically produce right living. Sometimes it produces excuses for wrong living. Don't let age be an excuse for inactivity. Be like Anna. Find out what you can do and do it. For some aging Christians, it's time to put the "saint" back into "senior saint."

The silver-haired
head is a
crown of glory.

—PROVERBS 16:31

APOLLOS

Teaching the Teachers

When a liberal theologian and an old deacon were asked to recite the twenty-third Psalm, the theologian's recitation was perfect. But the deacon's brought tears to everyone's eyes. Why? Because the

NAME: "Destroyer"
DATE: 1st Century AD
IDENTIFICATION: Eloquent Jewish teacher in the early church
STORY LINE: Apollos was instructed by Aquila and Priscilla in doctrine
READ IT IN THE BIBLE: Acts 18:1–28

theologian knew the psalm, but the old deacon knew the Shepherd.

You don't have to be a formally trained scholar to understand the Bible. Simple people who are intimate with God can teach scholars a thing or two about their Creator.

Priscilla and Aquila were like that. They were thoroughly familiar with God's Word. As they labored making tents they were taught by the best theologian around—the apostle Paul—and they needed this knowledge and understanding when Apollos arrived.

Apollos was a learned and eloquent Jew from Alexandria in Egypt. He was well–versed in the Old Testament, but as a disciple of John the Baptist, "he knew only the baptism of John" (Acts 18:25). Apollos was unaware of the teachings of Jesus the Messiah or His redemptive work. Apollos' message was accurate, but incomplete. So when he came to Ephesus, Priscilla and Aquila discretely took him aside and tutored him privately about Jesus. Apollos left Ephesus and traveled to Achaia where he skillfully refuted the Jews using his great knowledge of the Old Testament to prove that Jesus was the Messiah.

Apollos proves that even the scholarly can benefit from the insights of those who live close to the Lord. If you read and study your Bible daily, even the "experts" can benefit from your study. Don't be shy in sharing what you learn. You may be surprised at who needs to learn what you have discovered from faithfully mining the gold in God's Word.

ATHALIAH

Grandmas and Grandkids

Solomon said, "Children's children are the crown of old men" (Proverbs 17:6). My wife and I have twelve grandchildren whom we love dearly. Someone said that a woman begins to show her age at about the same time she begins to show pictures of her

NAME: "The Time of Jehovah"
DATE: 9th Century BC
IDENTIFICATION: Judah's only queen, daughter of Ahab and Jezebel
STORY LINE: Athaliah killed her grandsons, but God saved Joash
READ IT IN THE BIBLE: 2 Kings 11:1–16

grandchildren. I have watched my wife force perfect strangers to look at pictures of our grandchildren.

Not all grandmothers are as proud of their grandchildren as my wife is of ours. Take Athaliah, for example. She was married to King Jehoram (Joram), the son of Jehoshaphat, but her values were forged in her early years as the daughter of King Ahab of Israel and his notoriously wicked wife, Jezebel.

Like her mother, Athaliah worshiped the Canaanite god Baal and browbeat her husband to do the same. After Jehoram died, their son Ahaziah became king, and Athaliah exerted the same evil influence over him.

Ahaziah was killed after only one year, and Athaliah saw an opportunity to seize Judah's throne for herself. That required, however, destroying all the males in the royal family. Grandma Athaliah never flinched as she killed her own grandchildren to become Judah's only queen.

But Jehosheba, Jehoram's daughter, rescued one of her infant nephews, Joash, and hid him away for seven years. Finally, in a secret ceremony in the temple, Joash was crowned king, and when his surprised grandmother showed up she was executed.

There are two particularly memorable grandmothers in the Bible. Athaliah is remembered for her ruthlessness toward her grandchildren. Lois is remembered for having taught her grandson God's Word from childhood. One grandmother was a miserable failure, the other an undeniable success. What will you be remembered for?

AUGUSTUS

The Revered One

The date was March 15, 44 BC. The place was the Roman Senate. The event was the assassination of Julius Caesar. The result was that Caesar's 18-year-old heir, Gaius Octavianus, was called back from Greece where he had been studying. Caesar had adopted his

NAME: "The Revered One"
DATE: 1st Century BC
IDENTIFICATION: Julius Caesar's nephew, emperor at Jesus' birth
STORY LINE: Issued census that sent Mary and Joseph to Bethlehem
READ IT IN THE BIBLE: Luke 2:1–20

great-nephew Octavian as his son and named him heir in his will, but the Senate instead confirmed both Octavian and Caesar's powerful comrade Mark Antony to share power with Lepidus in a triumvirate. When Mark Antony was defeated by Octavian at the Battle of Actium, however, Octavian became the sole ruler of Rome until his death in AD 14. In 27 BC

Octavian took the title "Augustus," which means "the revered one," as a part of emperor worship that had been initiated by Julius Caesar.

When Caesar Augustus decreed that a taxation census should be made of everyone living in his empire, Joseph of Nazareth and Mary made their way to Bethlehem, and there was born Jesus, who is truly "the Revered One." One day ten thousand times ten thousand angels will fall before the Lamb of God and say, "Worthy is the Lamb who was slain to receive power and riches and wisdom, and strength and honor and glory and blessing!" (Revelation 5:12).

Caesar Augustus took the title "the revered one," but Jesus Christ earned the title by dying on Calvary's cross for your sins and mine. When you think today about whom you will revere, remember who is worthy. Only Jesus is worthy to be called "the Revered One." Give Him your adoration, your praise, and your reverence both in the way you worship and in the way you walk today.

BARNABAS

Encouragement

Two elderly men shared a hospital room—one by the window, the other by a far wall. Daily the one would describe what he saw out the window—children playing in the park, lovers walking hand-in-hand, swans on the lake. One day the man beside the

NAME: "Son of Encouragement"
DATE: 1st Century AD
IDENTIFICATION: Native of Cyprus named Joseph, partner with Paul
STORY LINE: Barnabas recruited Paul for ministry, then traveled with him
READ IT IN THE BIBLE: Acts 11:19–26; 13:1–5

window died, and the other man asked a nurse to push his bed near the window. Propping himself up on one elbow he looked out, and all he saw was the flat roof of the hospital building next to him. All those days his friend had been describing beautiful things just to encourage him. In the early church,

Barnabas would have been the man by the window. He was an encourager.

A Levite from the island of Cyprus, Barnabas' given name was Joseph or Joses, but everybody called him by his nickname, Barnabas, because it means "son of encouragement." Barnabas sold some land he owned and gave the money to the Jerusalem apostles to help the poor of the church. Later, when the church at Antioch needed a teacher, Barnabas journeyed there to instruct them in the Word. But when the task proved to be greater than one man could handle, he went to Tarsus to recruit some help. The man Barnabas recruited for ministry changed the face of the church. His name was Paul.

Are there people in your family, your church, your neighborhood, or your office who need encouragement today? Who will they turn to if not you? People crave encouragement. Strengthen them with your wisdom. Sustain them with your prayers. Stimulate them with your encouragement. Be the man by the window for those around you.

BARZILLAI

The Blessing of Friendship

Have you ever needed a friend when you were in a jam? Of course! Who hasn't? King David certainly did. When his son Absalom seized Israel's throne and drove David from Jerusalem, the king was on the run

NAME: "Made of Iron"
DATE: 9th Century BC
IDENTIFICATION: Member of the tribe of Gilead in Rogelim
STORY LINE: Barzillai showed kindness to David while the king was on the run
READ IT IN THE BIBLE: 2 Samuel 17:21–19:40

and needed a friend. Enter the generous octogenarian—Barzillai.

As David and his entourage crossed the river Jordan to seek safety at Mahanaim, an ancient town in Gilead near the river Jabbok, he was met by Barzillai and others who "brought beds and basins, earthen vessels and wheat, barley and flour, parched grain and beans, lentils and parched seeds, honey and curds, sheep and cheese"—supplies David needed but that he'd had to leave behind when he fled Jerusalem (2 Samuel 17:28–29).

After Absalom's rebellion ended and it was safe for David to return to the Holy City, Barzillai escorted him back across the Jordan. David wanted his friend to come with him to Jerusalem, but the eighty-year-old refused, saying he was an old man. Instead, Barzillai asked the king to take his servant Chimham and give him the opportunity to serve the king of Israel. This act of kindness probably was just another in a string of kindnesses done by Barzillai to many people.

Barzillai demonstrates that when God has blessed us, we ought to be a blessing to others. Sharing the goodness of God with others is the only way we get the full benefit of God's blessing to us. So if you know someone who is in need and you can help shoulder their burden, be a blessing to king or servant alike. To enjoy your blessings, be a blessing to others.

BATHSHEBA

Good From Evil

Only God could bring something so good out of something so evil.

Bathsheba was a beautiful woman, the wife of Uriah the Hittite, one of David's most loyal soldiers away on duty. One evening when King David saw her

NAME: "Daughter of the Promise"
DATE: 10th Century BC
IDENTIFICATION: Wife of Uriah the Hittite and then David the King
STORY LINE: David sinned with Bathsheba, had her husband killed
READ IT IN THE BIBLE: 2 Samuel 11:1–12:2

taking a bath, he did a stupid thing. Instead of looking away, he stared, lusted, and sent for Bathsheba to be brought to his palace. There he slept with her and she became pregnant. When Bathsheba told the king about the child, David did a deceitful thing. He had Uriah brought home so it would appear the child was his, but Uriah refused the pleasure of being home while his comrades were engaged in battle. Frustrated, David did an evil thing. He had Uriah sent to the frontlines specifically so he would be killed.

Eventually David confessed and repented of his sin. Bathsheba may not have been entirely innocent in this story either. But they paid a terrible price for their sin. They married but their child became sick and died.

Adultery can never be condoned, but leave it to God to bring something so good out of something so evil. David and Bathsheba later had seven sons, including Nathan and Solomon, who appear in the listing of the ancestry of Jesus Christ, as does Bathsheba herself, "who had been the wife of Uriah" (Matthew 1:6).

Sin is always defeating, debilitating, and deadly. But in His amazing grace, God often salvages something from our sin to bless us. Don't sin to be blessed, but don't despair when you do sin. Instead, cast yourself on God's mercy, as David and Bathsheba did, and allow Him to bring good from your evil.

CAIAPHAS

Success From Failure

At the peak of the reality TV craze, *American Idol* ruled the roost, especially *American Idol 2* when Ruben Studdard won with Clay Aiken coming in a close second. But in the months that followed, Clay appeared

NAME: "He Who Seeks"
DATE: 1st Century AD
IDENTIFICATION: High priest of Israel, son–in–law of Annas
STORY LINE: Caiaphas illegally tried and condemned Jesus
READ IT IN THE BIBLE: John 11:47–57; 18:1–28

to outshine Ruben with a top–selling single and appearances on programs like *The Tonight Show*.

Caiaphas knew what it was like to win and lose. He was appointed high priest of Israel in AD 18 by the Roman procurator, Valerius Gratus. Caiaphas became the official head of the Jewish State and presided over the Sanhedrin, Israel's highest court.

Next to the Roman governor, he was the land's most powerful man in Jesus' day.

But after Jesus raised Lazarus from the dead, Caiaphas and other Jewish leaders became alarmed at Jesus' increasing popularity. The Sanhedrin quickly called a meeting where Caiaphas demanded Jesus' death. He and the others actively plotted Jesus' arrest and held an illegal trial to condemn Him. Caiaphas was holding all the cards; in the contest the night before Jesus' crucifixion, you would have to consider him the winner. But in the days after Jesus' crucifixion, the real winner emerged.

In AD 36, Caiaphas was summarily removed from office by the proconsul Vitellus. Nothing more is ever heard from him. Jesus, on the other hand, lives and reigns forever, His impact is still being felt in your life and mine two thousand years later.

Success or failure isn't always evident from the scorecard. Sometimes our reaction to apparent defeat shows who the real winner is. When you don't come out on top, live as if you did. You'll make a difference anyway.

CALEB

Unfinished Business

The Nebraska Cornhuskers were college football's national champions in 1994. Their record was 13–0. They repeated as champs the next year with a 12–0 record. But in 1996 they stumbled, posting an 11–2 record. At the first home game of the 1997 season,

NAME: "Dog"
DATE: 15th Century BC
IDENTIFICATION: Son of Jephunneh, one of 12 spies sent into Canaan
STORY LINE: Caleb took on giants at age 85 to secure his inheritance
READ IT IN THE BIBLE: Numbers 13:1–33; Joshua 14:6–15

fans held placards reading: "We have unfinished business." That's just what they did. With another 13–0 season, the Huskers become national champions in 1997 for the third time in four years.

Caleb had some unfinished business of his own. Of the twelve spies sent on a reconnaissance mission into Canaan, only Joshua and Caleb returned with a positive report. The others confirmed that the land was lush and inviting, but there were giants in the land, the Anakim. So imposing were these descendants of Anak that the Israelites appeared as tiny grasshoppers by comparison. As a result, Israel followed the majority report, refused to enter the Promised Land, and wandered in the wilderness for forty years.

When Israel finally occupied Canaan, Caleb was an 85–year–old man. Still, he had unfinished business with the Anakim. He requested that his inheritance be the rugged, mountainous region around Hebron, the stronghold of the Anakim. Caleb said, "Give me this mountain . . . It may be that the Lord will be with me, and I shall be able to drive them out" (Joshua 14:12). What Israel feared to do forty years earlier, Caleb was eager to do as an octogenarian.

Do you have some unfinished business in your life? Something you failed to accomplish years ago? Don't let age be a deterrent to faith. Adopt Caleb's attitude. It may be that the Lord will be with you.

CLEOPAS

No Disappointment with Jesus

Sometimes disappointment is hard to hide. Friends and family let you down, and it's written all over your face. But what about when you think God lets you down? How do you beat back disappointment then?

NAME: "Renowned Father"
DATE: 1st Century AD
IDENTIFICATION: Christian from Emmaus, northwest of Jerusalem
STORY LINE: Cleopas encountered the risen Jesus on the road to Emmaus
READ IT IN THE BIBLE: Luke 24:1–35

Cleopas and a friend were glumly returning to Emmaus after a disappointing week in Jerusalem. They had gone to the Holy City for Passover, but they weren't prepared for what they encountered there— the shocking crucifixion of Jesus.

As true believers, they anticipated this was the Passover Jesus would declare Himself to be Messiah.

Instead He was humiliated and put to death. All their hopes were dashed. Their faith was in shambles.

As they trudged home, a stranger caught up with them and inquired what they were talking about. Not realizing it was Jesus, Cleopas related all the bizarre events of the week. Jesus responded by demonstrating from the Scriptures that every Bible writer had pointed to the events of this week; it was all part of God's plan. No sooner did they realize this was the resurrected Christ than He was gone.

Nothing could change their disappointment except the reality of the risen Christ. Nothing could make Cleopas and his friend retrace their steps to Jerusalem except news that was too exciting to keep to themselves. Jesus hadn't failed them. He is risen indeed!

If you find yourself disappointed with God, maybe you also need a fresh encounter with the resurrected Christ. Nothing is a better antidote to disappointed faith than to discover the reality that Jesus Christ is alive. We do not worship a dead Savior. We worship a living Lord. There is no disappointment in Jesus.

DANIEL

Taking A Stand

When Jim Neugent was offended by a television program that glorified homosexuality, he wrote to the network and objected, quoting some Scripture references. What he got back was a stinging rebuke from the network webmaster telling him to get his

NAME: "God is My Judge"
DATE: 6th Century BC
IDENTIFICATION: Jerusalem teen carried into Babylonian captivity
STORY LINE: Daniel became prominent in Babylon because of his character
READ IT IN THE BIBLE: Daniel 1:1–21; 6:1–28

nose out of the Bible and try thinking for himself instead of using an archaic book of stories as a crutch. Holding moral convictions in an immoral society isn't easy. It never has been.

Daniel was a teenager when Nebuchadnezzar abducted him. He and his friends were among Jerusalem's finest young men of noble birth, the crème de la crème. Nebuchadnezzar took them to Babylon to assimilate them into his culture. He afforded them elite status and invited them to eat the king's meat and drink the king's wine.

But Daniel refused the king's menu on principle and proposed an alternative. His friends and he would eat nothing but vegetables and drink nothing but water for ten days. They were convinced God would sustain them without the king's help. They stood up for what they believed.

When the test was over Daniel and his friends were not only sustained by God, they actually exceeded the others physically (Daniel 1:15), mentally (v. 17), spiritually (v. 17) and socially (v. 19).

Are you facing a situation today where you need to take a stand for what you believe? Maybe it's in the classroom or at work. Are you afraid you will suffer as a result? That's a normal concern, but learn from Daniel. Do the right thing and let God take care of the consequences. God never fails to bless integrity. Take a stand.

DAVID

The Quest of God

When President John F. Kennedy challenged American scientists to put a man on the moon, the race for space began. On July 20, 1969, Neil Armstrong took "one small step for man, one giant

NAME: "Beloved"
DATE: 10th Century BC
IDENTIFICATION: Son of Jesse, Israel's king, ancestor of Jesus
STORY LINE: Though not sinless, David was a man after God's own heart
READ IT IN THE BIBLE: 1 Samuel 13:13–14; 16:1–13

leap for mankind" and raised one of the first milestones in man's quest for space.

But did you know that God is on a quest, too? He's not looking to conquer space—that already belongs to Him. God is pursuing men and women who have a heart for Him. He is searching through "every tribe and tongue and people and nation" (Revelation 5:9), and when He discovers those whose hearts beat in sync with His, the result is always intimacy with the Almighty.

David was the kind of guy God was looking for. He admitted, "O God, You are my God; early will I seek You; my soul thirsts for You; my flesh longs for You, in a dry and thirsty land where there is no water" (Psalm 63:1).

When Samuel went to anoint one of Jesse's sons as Israel's king, God warned the prophet, "Do not look at his appearance or the height of his physical stature . . . for man looks at the outward appearance, but the LORD looks at the heart" (1 Samuel 16:7).

If you want to become more intimate with God, develop a healthy thirst for Him by meeting Him daily in His Word. Because God is on a quest for those thirsting for Him, you're already halfway there. Just make sure you have clean hands and a pure heart (Psalm 24:3–4). If you are clean before God and have a heart for Him, God will quench your thirst.

DEBORAH

The Right Woman for the Job

Of all the Fortune 500 companies, only eight today have female CEOs. Some are mega–companies like Hewlett-Packard, Xerox, Lucent Technologies, and Avon, but eight out of 500 is just over one percent.

NAME: "A Bee"
DATE: 13th Century BC
IDENTIFICATION: The fifth judge in Israel, the only female judge
STORY LINE: Victories of Deborah, a prophetess and a "mother of Israel"
READ IT IN THE BIBLE: Judges 4:1–5:31

Women in top leadership positions are rare. That's the way it was in the days of the judges, too.

Israel felt the crush of Jabin's hand for twenty years. This Canaanite king was one of the most powerful enemies Israel ever faced. He had nine hundred iron chariots, and his army seemed unstoppable. Israel needed a champion, but couldn't find one.

Sometimes the best man for the job is a woman. Deborah was a homemaker, wife of Lapidoth. They lived in the hill country of Ephraim, between Bethel and Ramah. But Deborah was also a prophetess. People from all around came to her for advice and to hear her dispense God's wisdom.

God impressed on Deborah that Barak should assemble an army of ten thousand men from Naphtali and Zebulun to stop Jabin. Barak agreed, but on the condition that Deborah go into battle with him. Barak led the swords of the troops but Deborah led their hearts. The poorly equipped Israelites defeated the Canaanites in the plain of Esdraelon. Not bad for a "mother in Israel" (Judges 5:7)

Does God have an inspired task for you today? Maybe it's raising godly kids. Perhaps it's organizing a support group for a noble cause. Whatever it is, God isn't looking for someone who's already a CEO. He's looking for dedicated men and women to rise up and meet challenges for Him. Ask God if you're one of them. Like Deborah, you may be the right person for the job.

DELILAH

Spying for the Enemy

During World War II, entertainer Josephine Baker helped the French Resistance by smuggling secret information written in invisible ink on her sheet music. Baker's fame made it possible for her to engage in espionage completely unsuspected.

NAME: "Dainty" or "Delicate"
DATE: 11th Century BC
IDENTIFICATION: Prostitute from valley of Sorek in Samson's day
STORY LINE: Woman tricked Samson into revealing source of strength
READ IT IN THE BIBLE: Judges 16:1–31

The most notorious spy of World War I was Mata Hari, a Dutch–born courtesan who was shot for espionage by the French on October 15, 1917.

But before Josephine Baker or Mata Hari, there was Delilah, the famous female spy in the Bible.

God chose Samson to deliver Israel from Philistine oppression. His uncanny strength led to stunning successes, and that prompted the Philistine rulers to offer Delilah a bribe to help them identify the source of Samson's great strength. Delilah's name means "delicate," and she delicately attempted to get Samson to reveal the source of his strength. Samson finally revealed that God gave him his strength and that his long hair was part of his Nazirite vow. This vow set him apart for God's special service, and if his hair was cut, his strength would be gone. As any skillful spy would do, Delilah lulled Samson to sleep, shaved his head, and delivered him bald and powerless to the Philistines.

I hope you don't have a Delilah in your life, but Satan has his spies everywhere. The only way to avoid them is to keep your eyes open, ask God for wisdom, and then stay away from those people most apt to lull you to sleep and steal your virtue. That was Solomon's advice to his son (Proverbs 4:14–16). It's still good advice today. God will give you strength to outlast Satan's spies.

DEMAS

Fumbling at the Goal Line

It was Super Bowl XXVII and millions were watching.
Dallas defensive lineman Leon Lett picked up a
fumble and rumbled toward the end zone. It was sure
to be his greatest moment in football. But as he
confidently slowed his 300–pound frame at the

NAME: "Popular"
DATE: 1st Century AD
IDENTIFICATION: Friend of Paul, Mark, Luke, and others at Rome
STORY LINE: Demas served in good company but abandoned his
    ministry
READ IT IN THE BIBLE: Colossians 4:10–18; Philemon 23–25; 2
    Timothy 4:9–18

one–yard line and victoriously raised the ball in the
air, Buffalo's Don Beebe took advantage of Lett's early
celebration and batted the ball out of his hand.
Instead of his most glorious moment, it became Lett's
most embarrassing.

Demas knew that feeling. He traveled extensively
with the great apostle Paul. Luke and he were with

Paul when he wrote to the Colossians (Colossians 4:14). Paul concluded his letter to Philemon with these salutations: "Epaphras, my fellow prisoner in Christ Jesus, greets you, as do Mark, Aristarchus, Demas, Luke, my fellow laborers" (Philemon 23–24).

Demas was in pretty good company. But something happened. Demas failed Paul right at the end. In Paul's final epistle his lament to Timothy was, "Be diligent to come to me quickly; for Demas has forsaken me, having loved this present world (2 Timothy 4:9–10).

Demas will forever be remembered as a deserter. We don't know what caused him to abandon Paul and the ministry. It may have been something very legitimate. Whatever it was, he loved it more than he loved serving God.

How sad when a faithful usher, small group leader, or worship team member ruins a lifetime of service by failing right at the end. Don't become a Demas. Hold onto the ball until you cross the goal line. "There remains therefore a rest for the people of God" (Hebrews 4:9). It's work now, rest then. Don't get them backwards.

There remains therefore a **rest** *for the people of God.*

—HEBREWS 4:9

DIONYSIUS

Intellect and Faith

Do you recognize the names Alvin Plantinga or Vern Poythress? How about William Lane Craig or J. P. Moreland? Maybe not, unless you are part of the academic community. But these men are part of a

NAME: "Divinely Touched"

DATE: 1st Century AD

IDENTIFICATION: Prominent man in Athens; member of the Areopagus

STORY LINE: Philosopher was saved when Paul preached on Mar's Hill

READ IT IN THE BIBLE: Acts 17:16–34

growing community of Christian scholars, brilliant men and women who have expressed faith in Christ.

Some people believe that intelligent faith is an oxymoron, like jumbo shrimp or bittersweet. But the scholars just mentioned disprove that. So did Dionysius.

Paul had just arrived in Athens and found the whole city engaged in various forms of idolatry, even intellectual idolatry. When the Greek philosophers heard Paul teaching about the resurrection, they wanted to debate him on the Areopagus, a bald hill near the famous Acropolis where the Athenian supreme court met. Here everyone sat together and exchanged their ideas. Here everyone was an equal in the Athenian democratic way.

But when it came time for Paul to speak, the smallish Jew stood up and told them they could know the God they considered to be unknown. He explained the Gospel to them, but as is often the case, there were few takers. Not many believed that day, but a few did, including Dionysius the Areopagite. An intellectual and brilliant philosopher came to Christ, not on the strength of his intellect, but on the strength of saving faith.

Paul said not many wise, not many mighty, not many noble are called to salvation (1 Corinthians 1:26), but he didn't say not any. Be faithful in your witness, even to those who may be your intellectual superiors. It's not intellect that saves; it's faith. Some will believe.

DORCAS

Investing in the Poor

Convinced that true religion not only converts sinners but also alleviates the sufferings of the poor, a passionate preacher named William Booth formed the Christian Revival Association. He wanted to meet the needs of London's East End, the poorest of the poor.

NAME: "Gazelle"

DATE: 1st Century AD

IDENTIFICATION: Joppa woman who was raised from the dead by Peter

STORY LINE: Also called Tabitha, she was known for deeds of charity

READ IT IN THE BIBLE: Acts 9:32–43

Two years later he renamed his group the Salvation Army, and one of the world's premier religious and humanitarian organizations was born.

The Bible has much to say about our duty to the poor. The Levitical law of gleaning made provision for always leaving some grain for the poor (Leviticus 23:22). Job made sure he cared for the poor (Job 31:16, 19,

22). Jesus blessed the poor (Luke 6:20). Paul took up a collection for the poor (Romans 15:26). Peter counseled us to remember the poor (Galatians 2:10), and James chastised anyone who treated the poor with less than respect (James 2:2–6). But the best teaching is always done by example.

Dorcas was a Christian woman from Joppa known for helping the poor (Acts 9:36–43). When she died everyone mourned her passing. But the apostle Peter was nearby at Lydda, and two men were sent to bring him to Joppa. Peter prayed and Dorcas, also called Tabitha, came back to life.

God doesn't promise such miracles for all who help the poor; He promises something better. "He who has pity on the poor lends to the LORD, and He will pay back what he has given" (Proverbs 19:17). Helping the poor is like handing your financial portfolio to God and asking Him to invest it for you. Seek out someone you can help today. It's seeking first the kingdom of God.

ERASTUS

Christians in Government

Politics is a dirty business. How often have you heard those words? But governmental service can be as much a ministry as serving in the local church. Paul said those who serve in positions of authority are "God's minister to you for good" (Romans 13:4). The mayor

NAME: "Beloved"
DATE: 1st Century AD
IDENTIFICATION: Corinth's city treasurer, director of public works in Paul's day
STORY LINE: Erastus was a city official who sent greetings to Rome
READ IT IN THE BIBLE: Romans 16:21–27

of the town is as much God's appointee as the pastor of the church.

Tucked away in the list of those who sent greetings along with Paul to the Christians at Rome was a government official. In some translations he is called a "chamberlain," which originally was a royal official in charge of the private quarters of the king. But with time, chamberlains took on other official duties as well. Perhaps that's how Erastus became the treasurer of his hometown, Corinth (Romans 16:23).

In 1929 archaeologists from the American School of Classical Studies found a Latin inscription on a marble paving stone at Corinth with the name Erastus on it. Whether it was the same man or not we cannot tell, but Paul's friend apparently was well known to the believers in Rome.

The fact that Erastus could serve the Corinthian government and the Lord at the same time is not surprising. God never intended politics to be a dirty business. Government service has always been honorable when it honors God. Perhaps if more Christians like Erastus entered government service, politics wouldn't be such a dirty business.

Take some time today to pray for the leaders of your nation, your local government, and your town. And pray for your city treasurer too. You might just be praying for another Christian like yourself.

ESAU

Making Rash Decisions

We know three things about Esau when he was born. First, he was the older twin brother of Jacob. Second, his body was very red at birth. And third, he was a hairy baby. One translation says, "He was covered

NAME: "Hairy"
DATE: 20th Century BC
IDENTIFICATION: Twin brother of Jacob, ancestor of the Edomites
STORY LINE: Esau impulsively sold his birthright to Jacob for stew
READ IT IN THE BIBLE: Genesis 25:21–34

with so much hair that one would think he was wearing a piece of clothing" (Genesis 25:25 NLT).

Because Esau was the firstborn son, he enjoyed the privilege of a birthright that included a double inheritance, the expectation of becoming head of the family, and a special blessing from the parents. But Esau seemed to place little value on his privilege.

His casual approach to the rights of the firstborn caused him to make a very foolish decision.

Esau was a skillful hunter. One day he came in from the field where he had been hunting wild game, and he was famished. His twin, Jacob, had prepared some tasty stew. So callous was Esau's esteem for his birthright, and so crafty was Jacob, that when the hunter asked for some stew, the chef said, "Sell me your birthright." Impulsively, Esau made a decision that impacted the rest of his life and generations to come. He sold all the rights of the firstborn to Jacob for one measly bowl of stew.

Rash decisions can ruin your life. That's why who you choose to marry, where you choose to live and work, and even the church you choose to fellowship with can alter your future. Never make such decisions callously. Bathe them in prayer. Seek the counsel of godly people whom you trust. Give yourself time to think biblically, rationally, and wisely. Make godly decisions and you will make good decisions.

EBED-MELECH

Using What You Have

I have a missionary friend who would be considered "old school." Not that he doesn't use modern technology; he does. But in more than forty-five years in Peru he has learned to be very resourceful. Give him some duct tape and bailing wire and he can fix anything.

NAME: "Servant of the King"
DATE: 7th Century BC
IDENTIFICATION: An Ethiopian eunuch who served in King Zedekiah's court
STORY LINE: Ebed-Melech rescued the prophet Jeremiah from a well
READ IT IN THE BIBLE: Jeremiah 38:1-28

One of the most resourceful men in the Bible was Ebed-Melech. He was an Ethiopian eunuch. (No, not the one you know in Acts 8.) Ebed-Melech is the Old Testament Ethiopian eunuch.

When Jeremiah pronounced God's judgment on Judah, it was unappreciated. King Zedekiah's princes were angered. They wanted to get rid of this prophet who predicted bad things for their father, so they lowered him by ropes into an old well. There was nothing in the pit but mud, and Jeremiah quickly sank in the mire. But Ebed–Melech told the king what the princes did and received his permission to rescue Jeremiah. Ebed–Melech rounded up thirty men to help him pull the prophet from the mud. But so thoughtful and resourceful was this eunuch that he took what he had on hand—old clothes and old rags—and lowered them to Jeremiah so the aging prophet could put them under his armpits and prevent abrasion while being pulled out. It wasn't pretty, but it worked.

What do you have lying around that you could use to serve the Lord? An old computer? A hammer? A frying pan? Whatever it is, God can use whatever you've got. All you have to do is be willing and on the lookout for someone stuck in the mud.

EHUD

God's Southpaw

Do you know what presidents James A. Garfield, Harry Truman, Gerald Ford, Ronald Reagan, George Bush, and Bill Clinton have in common? They are all left–handed! That's also true for baseball greats Ted

NAME: "He Who Praises"
DATE: 14th Century BC
IDENTIFICATION: Left–handed Benjamite who delivered Israel of the Moabites
STORY LINE: Ehud killed Eglon, king of Moab who had menaced Jericho
READ IT IN THE BIBLE: Judges 3:12–30

Williams, Babe Ruth, Steve Carlton, Sandy Cofax, Ty Cobb, Whitey Ford, Reggie Jackson, and Stan Musial.

Ehud was also a lefty, the only left–handed judge in Israel. But like presidents and baseball players, he didn't allow being a sinistral (the Latin for left–handed is "sinister") get him down. In fact, in his case, being left–handed was the key to his success.

Eglon was the king of Moab. For eighteen years he

harassed the people of Israel, especially around the city of Jericho. For eighteen years he forced them to pay tribute to him. Ehud decided to put an end to it. He forged an iron dagger, and then when he took Israel's tribute to Eglon, he requested a private meeting with the Moabite king. When Eglon's guards searched Ehud, they didn't think to look for a weapon that could be drawn easily by a lefty, so he was able to surprise the king by using his left hand to sink the dagger deep into Eglon's stomach. He escaped through the doors that led to the porch. Later, Ehud rallied the Israelites west of the Jordan River to encircle the Moabite troops before they could return to Moab. Israel's enemy was trapped and destroyed by a left–handed leader.

Sometimes being a little different can be a good thing. It was the fact that Ehud was a southpaw that introduced eighty years of peace in Israel. View your difference as a blessing, and it could take you a long way.

ELEAZAR

Waiting Your Turn

Do you ever get tired of waiting your turn? Maybe you've been assistant leader of your Bible study group for years, and it's beginning to look like you'll never be the leader. Perhaps you're third in line to run the family business, and you want to make it the Lord's

NAME: "God is My Helper"

DATE: 15th Century BC

IDENTIFICATION: Aaron's third son, high priest and chief of the Levites

STORY LINE: Eleazar became leader when brothers Nadab and Abihu died

READ IT IN THE BIBLE: Exodus 6:23–25; Numbers 3:1–4, 32; 20:22–29

business. Your two older siblings, however, just want to make money. If you're getting impatient, read on.

Aaron had four sons—Nadab, Abihu, Eleazar, and Ithamar. Imagine being Eleazar. You had a heart for God. You wanted to serve Him. But it appeared as if you would never get your big break.

But God honors those who stay ready to serve and are patient. Nadab and Abihu offered unconsecrated fire on the altar, and both of them were struck dead. Without warning, Eleazar's number came up.

Eleazar supervised the tabernacle sanctuary and all its vessels. Before Aaron died, Eleazar ascended Mount Hor with his father and his uncle Moses, who invested him with Aaron's high priestly garments. Eleazar served as high priest during the remainder of Moses' life. Joshua was commissioned by Moses in the presence of Eleazar, who served as high priest throughout Joshua's leadership. He assisted Joshua in allotting the land of Canaan among the twelve tribes.

God used Eleazar to do much more, but none of this would have happened had he gotten impatient or failed to remain usable to the Lord while he waited his turn. So if you're anxious about getting your turn to serve, don't be. Be active. Be ready. Be patient. Be usable. Your day will come.

ELI

Being God's Recruiter

Have you women noticed that men are notoriously hard of hearing? When our wives talk to us, they accuse us of having selective hearing—hearing only what we want to hear. Sometimes we do that with God too. That's what Eli did.

NAME: "Lifting Up"
DATE: 11th Century BC
IDENTIFICATION: Priest at Shiloh who raised the prophet Samuel
STORY LINE: Eli raised Samuel, but he initially discouraged Samuel from heeding God's call
READ IT IN THE BIBLE: 1 Samuel 3:1–21

Eli was a good man, a pious priest at Shiloh in the period of the judges. Shiloh was about ten miles north of Jerusalem, but every now and then, Eli's misconnects with God were so significant that they put Him much more distant than that.

Eli blessed the childless Hannah who had been praying for a son. Later, when Hannah gave birth to

Samuel, she brought him to Eli to raise as she had promised God. Eli was to nurture Samuel for service in the sanctuary, but when Samuel needed Eli the most, Eli was hard of hearing.

Three times God called to young Samuel to commission him in ministry, and two out of the three times Eli the old priest told him to go back to bed. Only the third time were Eli's ears sensitive to what God wanted to say to Samuel.

When you raise your children or grandchildren to be open to following the Lord in lifetime service, don't turn a deaf ear when they need you. Sometimes they look to us for help in understanding and confirming God's call on their lives, and yet too many parents and grandparents listen with "Eli ears" and respond with the modern equivalent of, "Go back to bed." When God is moving in the lives of those you mentor, don't be hard of hearing. Listen with them. Sometimes listen for them. But always listen.

ELIAB

Through God's Eyes

People often have a hard time looking beyond the obvious. In sports, for example, winning seems to be everything. In reflecting on her six consecutive Wimbledon titles (1982–1987), however, tennis star

NAME: "God is My Father"
DATE: 10th Century BC
IDENTIFICATION: Oldest son of Jesse, brother of David the King
STORY LINE: Jesse's firstborn was not God's pick to become king
READ IT IN THE BIBLE: 1 Samuel 16:1–13

Martina Navratilova said, "The moment of victory is much too short to live for that and nothing else."

It shouldn't surprise us that God sees things differently than we do. He views life as more than winners and losers. Often those we see as the winners are losers to Him. God's ways are not our ways; His thoughts not our thoughts (Isaiah 55:8–9).

Nowhere in the Bible is this contrast sharper than in the selection of Israel's king. Saul proved to be a disappointment as king, so God sent the prophet Samuel to the house of Jesse in Bethlehem to anoint a new one. Jesse paraded his oldest before Samuel. When the prophet saw Eliab he said, "Surely the Lord's anointed is before Him!" But God didn't agree.

Next came Jesse's son Abinadab, but he wasn't right either. After him in quick succession came Shammah, Nethanel, Raddai, and Ozem. None was God's choice. David, the youngest son, wasn't even presented until Samuel asked if Jesse had any more sons.

God explained the way He sees things: "For man looks at the outward appearance, but the LORD looks at the heart" (1 Samuel 16:7). David was a man after God's own heart; the others had plenty of strength and talent, but they did not have a heart for God. If you want to be a winner with God, don't live for the victory of the moment. Live for more. Have a heart for God and live for eternity.

ELIEZER

Choosing Your Mate

Faithfulness is one of the chief character traits of good and godly people, but this quality seems to be in shorter supply all the time. One powerful example of faithfulness in the Bible is a man named Eliezer.

NAME: "God is My Helper"
DATE: 22nd Century BC
IDENTIFICATION: Native of Damascus, Abraham's chief steward
STORY LINE: Followed Abraham's guidelines for finding Isaac's wife
READ IT IN THE BIBLE: Genesis 24:1–67

Eleven biblical characters own that name, but Abraham's servant well demonstrates faithfulness. If Abraham had never had a son, Eliezer of Damascus would have been his heir. But Abraham did have a son, and when he wanted to find a wife for Isaac, Abraham turned to his faithful Syrian servant.

The principles followed by Eliezer in searching for Isaac's bride are still valid today. First, set divine guidelines for choosing a mate. Abraham said, "You will not take a wife for my son from the daughters of the Canaanites" (v. 3). Men and women of faith are to marry men and women of faith (2 Corinthians 6:14,15). Second, seek divine goodness. Eliezer prayed, "O LORD God of my master Abraham, please give me success this day" (v. 12). Third, request divine confirmation of your choice. Eliezer asked God to verify his choice of Isaac's bride by having her both offer to give him a drink and his camels as well (vv. 13,14). You know how thirsty camels can be. And finally, always thank God when the right person is found. It was love at first sight when Isaac and Rebekah saw each other (vv. 63–67).

Eliezer was faithful in following his master's wishes. If you are faithful in following God's wishes, you won't go wrong in choosing a life's mate. Following divine guidelines is so much better than taking a leap into the dark.

ELIHU

Knowing God or Knowing About God

Ian was a fifth–year seminary student. He read the Dutch theologians, the Puritans and anyone else plumbing the depths of God. But Ian had a problem. While he could hold his own in any theological argument, quote the most obscure sources, and generally

NAME: "He is My God"
DATE: Unknown; early BC
IDENTIFICATION: Son of Brachial, a Bustier, would–be comforter of Job
STORY LINE: Elihu failed to answer Job's questions convincingly
READ IT IN THE BIBLE: Job 32:1–12; 34:1–12

bore you to tears, he didn't have much heart. He knew all about God, but he didn't know God very well.

Ian is not the first young man to experience this inadequacy. Elihu, the youngest of Job's so–called "comforters," had the same problem. He is called the son of Brachial the Bustier of the family of Ram. Like Job's other friends—Eliphaz, Bildad, and Zophar—

Elihu was probably from Transjordan, the area east of the Jordan River, southeast of the Promised Land.

Elihu was slow to join the theological discussion between Job and his friends. He deferred to their age and let them speak first. But his ego led him to believe that their arguments to Job were unsubstantial and unconvincing. He would nail Job on the belief that suffering was a form of God's discipline, and that would be the slam–dunk end of the argument. But when Job cross–examined his young friend, Elihu failed to give convincing answers to Job's questions.

Knowing God and merely knowing about God are two very different things. Elihu had formulated all the theological answers, but it was Job who was blameless and upright, the man who feared God and shunned evil. When the roof came crashing in, Job knew that survival was a matter of faith in God's character, not a matter of having all the answers. Elihu had arguments; Job had faith. Which do you have?

ELIJAH

Society Erosion

When British anthropologist John D. Unwin conducted an in–depth study of eighty civilizations, he made some amazing discoveries. Examining four thousand years of history, he found a common thread running through all the civilizations. Each society

NAME: "Jehovah is My God"

DATE: 9th Century BC

IDENTIFICATION: Prophet who shaped the thinking of the Northern Kingdom

STORY LINE: Elijah defeated the prophets of Baal on Mt. Carmel

READ IT IN THE BIBLE: 1 Kings 18:16–46

began with strong moral values and a heavy emphasis on the family. Over the years, however, the conservative mind–set became more liberal and moral values declined. When values declined, families suffered. In all eighty civilizations, the fall of the nation was related to the fall of the family. In most cases, that civilization fell within one generation of the decay of the biblical family unit.

Societies never collapse overnight. They only collapse after their foundations are eroded year after year, bad decision after bad decision. Elijah the prophet knew that, and he saw it happening in Israel. Something had to be done.

Elijah's preaching emphasized unconditional loyalty to God. That was in direct conflict with the practices of king Ahab, who married Jezebel, daughter of Ethbaal, king of Tyre. Together Ahab and Jezebel were eroding the virtues held dear by the people of God and were implementing practices contrary to God's Law. Elijah called for a Mt. Carmel summit. He challenged four hundred fifty prophets of Baal to a contest. One challenge, winner takes all. "The God who answers by fire, He is God" (1 Kings 18:24).

God used Elijah to spotlight the kinds of issues that erode a godly society. Those same issues are at work today in our society. Pray that God will again answer by fire and stop the erosion of virtues and values in the world. He did it before; He can do it again.

ELISHA

Living Under Tall Shadows

Have you ever walked behind someone who cast a pretty tall shadow? Elisha did. He had the unenviable task of following Elijah, the great man of God who challenged the prophets of Baal and won. Later Elijah passed by Elisha plowing with a team of oxen and

NAME: "God is My Salvation"

DATE: 9th Century BC

IDENTIFICATION: Successor to Elijah, had 50–year ministry in Northern Kingdom

STORY LINE: Elisha learned from the master, then equaled his work

READ IT IN THE BIBLE: 1 Kings 19:15–21; 2 Kings 2:1–22

threw his mantle over the younger man's shoulders. By this Elisha knew he was called of God to be Elijah's successor.

In 1990, when the board of Back to the Bible International invited me to be president and Bible teacher for a worldwide ministry, I found myself walking in the footsteps of two giants—Theodore Epp and Warren Wiersbe. I know how Elisha felt.

But all who follow great men and women have to take hold of God's promise to Joshua, a man who followed a pretty great leader himself. God reminded him, "As I was with Moses, so I will be with you. I will not leave you nor forsake you" (Joshua 1:5). God helps each of us carve out our own ministries for Him.

Instead of following his mentor's example as a loner and outsider, Elisha worked within the system as a trusted advisor and sometimes critic of four kings—Jehoram, Jehu, Jehoahaz, and Joash. His ministry lasted approximately fifty years. He received a double portion of Elijah's spirit and performed twice as many miracles as did Elijah. So much of God was in Elisha that when a corpse was placed in Elisha's tomb, it came back to life as it touched the prophet's bones (2 Kings 13:21).

Never fear to follow the great ones. You don't have to fill their shoes, only follow their footsteps. God will give you your own shoes to fill.

EUNICE

Raising Godly Kids By Yourself

Living a life that pleases God isn't always easy—especially if your spouse chooses not to join you in that life. That was the case with Eunice. Although her name is Greek, she was a Jewess trying to raise her son without the help of a godly husband. Eunice's

NAME: "Good Victory"
DATE: 1st Century AD
IDENTIFICATION: daughter of Lois; mother of Timothy
STORY LINE: Jewess raising her son in Lystra (modern Turkey)
TODAY'S SCRIPTURE READING: 2 Timothy 1:1–5; 3:14–16;
    Acts 16:1–6

husband was a Greek and not a believer in Jesus. She faced the double whammy of a marriage challenged ethnically as well as religiously.

Did she abandon hope in raising her son Timothy? Not at all. With the help of her believing mother, Eunice diligently shaped young Timothy's life for the Lord. She taught him God's Word from the moment he could understand, and it stuck with him in later years. Paul counseled Timothy to "continue in the things which you have learned and been assured of, knowing from whom you have learned them, and that from childhood you have known the Holy Scriptures . . ." (2 Timothy 3:14–15). Eunice did not have the joy of leading her son to the Lord; Paul did that. He refers to Timothy as "my beloved and faithful son in the Lord" and his "true son in the faith." But Eunice did know that the seeds of faith she planted in her son would bear fruit, and they did, in a big way.

You can do the same. If you're a single parent or if your spouse doesn't share your faith, with God's help you can fill the spiritual role of both parents. Just be faithful in teaching God's Word to your children and setting an example for them. You never know, you may have a future Timothy sitting on your knee.

FELIX

Dealing with Delays

Do you enjoy delays? When you look at the departure board in the airport and see your flight is delayed, do you go ballistic? Is there a better way for a Christian to respond to delay? Paul's years with Felix show us there is.

NAME: "Happy"
DATE: 1st Century AD
IDENTIFICATION: Roman governor of Judea before whom Paul appeared
STORY LINE: Felix was moved by Paul's testimony, but did not convert
READ IT IN THE BIBLE: Acts 24:1–27

Felix was the unscrupulous Roman governor of Judea, capable of committing any crime imaginable. Paul was sent to Felix in Caesarea when he was arrested in Jerusalem for disturbing the peace. His accusers, however, delayed five days before they arrived. An orator named Tertullus proceeded to accuse Paul, but the apostle refuted each charge. Paul should have been freed then, but Felix postponed his judgment until he could hear from Lysias, the tribune. Several days later, Paul was brought before Felix a second time where he gave his testimony as a Christian. Felix admitted being moved, but he dismissed Paul again, indicating they would talk on a more convenient day. Felix sent for Paul on several occasions, but kept him in prison for two years. Paul finally was taken to Rome to appear before Caesar.

During these unjustified delays, did you notice what Paul did? Did you read what he said? Nothing. He never lost his cool. He never complained about wrongful imprisonment. He simply maintained a positive witness before the contemptible Felix.

When you are faced with annoying delays, ask yourself whether it's more important for you rush to the next thing or to maintain a Christian testimony to those who delay you. Remember, we have all eternity to enjoy the rewards of godly living, but only a few hours before sunset to win them. Don't let delays defeat you.

GAMALIEL

Unstoppable

"If God be for us, who can be against us?" Paul's logic in Romans 8:31 was inspired, but it may have reflected his training as well. Another great rabbi also believed this.

NAME: "Recompense of God"
DATE: 1st Century AD
IDENTIFICATION: Famous member of the Sanhedrin, teacher of Paul
STORY LINE: Advised the Sanhedrin to use moderation on the apostles
READ IT IN THE BIBLE: Acts 5:17–42

Gamaliel was a Jewish scholar in the first century AD. He had a particularly bright and eager student named Saul of Tarsus (Acts 22:3). From Gamaliel Saul learned the Law and the traditions of the rabbis. Two influential Pharisaic rabbinical schools had evolved by this time, one by Hillel and the other by Shammai. Gamaliel is considered to be the grandson of Hillel.

Gamaliel was not only a member of the Sanhedrin,

but he served as its president during the reigns of Roman emperors Tiberius, Caligula, and Claudius. Once when the high priest hauled the apostles before the Sanhedrin and ordered them to quit preaching in Jesus' name, Peter said, "We ought to obey God rather than men." Incensed, the Sanhedrin wanted to kill the apostles until the cool-headed Gamaliel rose and advised, "Keep away from these men and let them alone; for if this plan or this work is of men, it will come to nothing; but if it is of God, you cannot overthrow it" (Acts 5:38,39).

Hudson Taylor delighted in saying, "God's work, done in God's way, will never lack God's supply." Paul said, "If God is for us, who can be against us?" Gamaliel said, "If it is of God, you cannot overthrow it."

If you have clean hands and a pure heart, and if you have a green light from God, then no one will be able to keep you from accomplishing His work. Rejoice in that, and live like it.

GIDEON

Faith is Better Than Fleeces

Is it a good idea to set up the parameters within which God may work? How often have you said something like, "If Shawn calls me back, I'll know this is the person I should marry"? Sounds a bit risky, doesn't it?

NAME: "Warrior" or "Destroyer"
DATE: 12th Century BC
IDENTIFICATION: Son of Joash, military hero and spiritual leader in Israel
STORY LINE: Gideon was a man of anemic faith that grew to valor
READ IT IN THE BIBLE: Judges 6:1–7:15

Gideon took that risk. The Midianites had badgered Israel for seven years, raiding their sheep pens and stealing grain from their fields. Finally, the Angel of the Lord appeared to Gideon and commissioned him to lead an army against Midian, but Gideon balked. He wanted proof, a sign, anything that would confirm what God had clearly told him.

God put up with Gideon's feeble faith by zapping

some meat and unleavened bread. Gideon wanted more. He laid a fleece on the ground and asked God to do the extraordinary—place morning dew only on the fleece and leave the ground around it dry. God did so. Gideon still wanted more. God reversed the process the next morning. Gideon finally agreed to fight, but often continued to question the wisdom of God.

Gideon became a military hero and spiritual leader in Israel, but his initial need for God to prove everything to him before he would believe was not the divine design for discerning God's will. Today, we know God's way because we know His will, and we know His will because we know His Word. When God gives you clear direction in His Word, don't question Him, don't ask for some confirmation of your own design, just trust Him. Hebrews 11:6 says that without faith it is impossible to please God. Gideon learned that the hard way.

Without faith it is impossible to please God.

— Hebrews 11:6

HABAKKUK

Let God Be God

Recently, Barna Research polled over one thousand people and asked: "If you could ask God one question, what would it be?" Surprisingly, no one asked, "Do You really exist?" or "Is the Bible really

true?" Most people wanted to know why they lost their jobs or where God was on September 11, 2001.

People have been asking "Where were You, God?" for a long time. Habakkuk was a prophet in the reigns of Josiah and Jehoiakim, when the Chaldeans were menacing the nations around them. He questioned, "O LORD, how long shall I cry, and You will not hear? . . . Why do You show me iniquity, and cause me to see trouble? . . . The law is powerless, and justice never goes forth" (Habakkuk 1:2–4).

Habakkuk couldn't understand why God would not judge evil. "Are You not from everlasting, O Lord my God, my Holy One? . . . Why do You look on those who deal treacherously, and hold Your tongue . . ." (Habakkuk 1:12–13).

Habakkuk was learning what we all must learn: God is slow to anger and of great compassion (Nehemiah 9:17; Psalm 103:8; 145:8; Joel 2:13; Jonah 4:2; Nahum 1:3). He tempers His holiness and justice with His mercy and love. What Habakkuk finally had to do was acquiesce to the timetable of God and just let God be God.

If it appears God is moving too slowly in taking care of the evil in your world, do what Habakkuk did—pray. Focus on the unique mixture of God's justice and compassion. Trust God to make all things right in His own time. And then let God be God.

HAGGAI

Don't Lose Your Momentum

Leonardo da Vinci failed to complete his painting of the *Adoration of the Magi* because when he stopped, he couldn't get started again. Often it's more difficult to start again than it is just to keep going. Sometimes

NAME: "Festive"
DATE: 6th Century BC
IDENTIFICATION: Old Testament prophet who paired with Zechariah in ministry
STORY LINE: Haggai encouraged the exiles to complete the Temple
READ IT IN THE BIBLE: Haggai 1:1–15; Ezra 5:1–5

when momentum is lost, it's lost forever. No one knew that better than the prophet Haggai.

When the Babylonian Empire fell to the Persian king Cyrus in 539 B.C., Cyrus decreed that the house of God at Jerusalem could be rebuilt, and he released the Jews from captivity so they could return to their homeland and get on with their lives. Wave after wave of immigration began, and the reconstruction of the

Temple started almost immediately. But something happened. The people met with stiff opposition and became discouraged. Soon the work on the Temple stopped, and the people began to channel their money and their energies into refurbishing their own houses. For sixteen years nothing was done in rebuilding the Temple.

But in 520 BC, Haggai and his fellow prophet Zechariah urged the people to get back to work on God's house. "Consider your ways" was Haggai's constant plea, and it worked. The people began building again and the Temple was completed five years later, about 515 BC (Ezra 5:1).

Momentum is important in politics, in sports, and in ministry. If you have lost your momentum for God and are sitting on the sidelines or are channeling your energies elsewhere, "consider your ways." The work God has for you to do can only be done by you. Ask God to help you get going again, and this time keep it going.

HANNAH

Keeping Your Promises

In 2001, the Chicago White Sox held a "Cancer Survivors Night." Before the game, Jose Canseco spoke to four hundred fifty cancer patients and promised to hit a couple of home runs for them. True to his word, the first two balls pitched to him left the park.

NAME: "Gracious"
DATE: 11th Century BC
IDENTIFICATION: Wife of Elkanah, mother of the prophet Samuel
STORY LINE: When barren Hannah bore a son, he was dedicated to God
READ IT IN THE BIBLE: 1 Samuel 1:1–2:21

Hannah's promise to God, and the way she kept it, proves that one thing you can give and still keep is your word.

The wife of Elkanah, Hannah had a miserable life. First, Elkanah had two wives, which always proves to be an aggravation. Second, Hannah had no children, which was a strain on her maternal instincts. And finally, Elkanah's other wife, Peninnah, constantly hassled Hannah for being childless. But Hannah was patient and laid her burden before the Lord in prayer. She promised that if God gave her a son, she would give him back in lifetime service.

God honored Hannah's prayer, and she honored her promise. In time, Hannah gave birth to Samuel, and when he was weaned she and Elkanah took him to Shiloh, where they entrusted him to Eli the priest. It must have been heart–rending, but Hannah gave her son to the Lord as she had promised.

The Bible doesn't require you to make promises to God, but if you do, you are required to honor them. When you do, you discover that God's reward is always greater than your promise. Hannah had three more sons and two daughters (1 Samuel 2:21). Samuel made his mother's heart proud by becoming a faithful man of God. Promises are only as dependable as the individuals who make them, so show yourself dependable to God and enjoy His blessings.

HEROD THE GREAT

God is in Control

The long war against God has been as fierce as it has been constant. Since his personal rebellion, Satan has amassed an army dedicated to thwarting the purposes of God. We still wrestle against principalities and powers, the rulers of the darkness of this age.

NAME: "Song of a Hero"
DATE: 1st Century BC
IDENTIFICATION: Jewish king who ruled Judea when Jesus was born
STORY LINE: Herod slew Bethlehem's infant boys in order to kill Jesus
READ IT IN THE BIBLE: Matthew 2:1–23

One of Satan's soldiers was Herod the Great. With the support of Mark Antony, Herod managed to get himself appointed king of Judea by the Roman Senate in 40 BC. He was a ruthless fighter, a subtle diplomat, and a prolific builder. His crowning achievement was the rebuilding of the Temple in Jerusalem. Rabbinic literature says, "He who has not seen the Temple of Herod has never seen a beautiful building."

Herod enjoyed being king until wise men from the East arrived and asked, "Where is He who has been born King of the Jews?" (Matthew 2:2). Herod must have said to himself, I thought I was the king of the Jews. When the chief priests and scribes informed him that the Savior and Messiah would be born in Bethlehem, the ruthless Herod put to death all the male children of Bethlehem from two years old and younger, hoping to kill Jesus.

Neither Herod nor any other of Satan's henchmen can thwart the plan of God. The Almighty said, "I have spoken it; I will also bring it to pass. I have purposed it; I will also do it" (Isaiah 46:11). When it seems that Satan's power and influence are becoming pervasive, don't worry. God is still in control and He has the devil on a short leash. God will prevail. You can count on it.

HERODIAS

Silencing Voices of Morality

Indiana state trooper Ben Endres was dismissed by his State Police supervisor after refusing to report for duty at the Blue Chip Casino. As a Christian, Endres felt his presence would appear to condone gambling and drinking.

NAME: "Song of a Hero"
DATE: 1st Century AD
IDENTIFICATION: Granddaughter of Herod Great, wife of Philip and Antipas
STORY LINE: Hated John the Baptist, demanded his head on a platter
READ IT IN THE BIBLE: Matthew 14:1–12

Casualties of immorality often include those who speak out against it. Their voices are suppressed by sinners and only lukewarmly supported by saints. John the Baptist was one of those voices. He felt the heat of Herodias' hatred because he dared to be incensed at her sin.

Herodias, granddaughter of Herod the Great, was

married to her father's brother, Phillip. Around AD 29, Phillip's half-brother Herod Antipas took a trip to Rome, and on the way he visited Herod Phillip at his coastal home in Palestine. Antipas became infatuated with Herodias, Phillip's wife. On his return from Rome, Herod Antipas and Herodias divorced their spouses and eloped. John the Baptist openly denounced this scandalous marriage, and it cost him dearly.

Herodias immediately plotted John's death. Her daughter Salome danced seductively for Antipas at a banquet, and he promised her anything she wanted. Following her mother's wishes, Salome asked for the head of John the Baptist on a platter, and she got it (John 14:11). John was murdered at Herod's Machaerus fortress on the eastern shore of the Dead Sea.

Speaking out against sin is never popular and can be deadly. Pray for those who speak out against contemporary immorality. Pray that their voices will not be silenced by the hatred of those who have contempt for righteousness. And when the opportunity comes for you to stand against sin, join those who are voices in the wilderness.

HEZEKIAH

Learning How to Pray

That Hezekiah could be born to Ahaz, one of Judah's ungodly kings, can only be the grace of God. Hezekiah demonstrated his devotion to Jehovah by immediately reopening the Temple doors his father had closed, destroying high places and pagan altars,

NAME: "Strength of Jehovah"
DATE: 8th Century BC
IDENTIFICATION: 13th king of Southern Kingdom; son of Ahaz
STORY LINE: Good king who instituted major religious reforms in Judah
READ IT IN THE BIBLE: 2 Kings 18:28–19:1–19, 35–37

and doing much more. Hezekiah's reforms were as widespread as they were deep.

But when Sennacherib, king of Assyria, invaded Palestine and threatened to destroy Jerusalem, Hezekiah demonstrated his true intimacy with God. As soon as he received an ultimatum letter, Hezekiah took it to the Temple and spread it before the Lord. His prayer for deliverance, recorded in 2 Kings 19:14–19, is a model for us today.

Hezekiah's prayer was *spontaneous* (v. 14). There was no Plan B—there was only God. He never considered anything else. Hezekiah's prayer was *reverent* (v. 15). He didn't begin with his need, though it was urgent; he began by praising God. Hezekiah's prayer was *personal* (v. 16). He spoke to Jehovah as an intimate friend, inviting Him to bend His ear out of heaven and hear the king's desperate prayer. Hezekiah's prayer was *informative* (vv. 17–18). God loves for us to provide information about our specific needs, not so He knows how desperate our situation is, but so we know. Finally, Hezekiah's prayer was *direct* (v. 19). His request was to the point: "O Lord . . . save us."

If you're having trouble getting through to God, pattern your prayers after Hezekiah's. Maybe you're rushing too soon to your request. Spend some time enjoying God's presence first, as Hezekiah did, and watch how He answers your prayers.

HUSHAI

Secret Agent for the King

When Bryan Johnson caught Cal Ripken Jr.'s home run that broke Lou Gehrig's consecutive games streak, he knew he could have sold it for thousands of dollars. Instead he gave it to Ripken saying, "It will

NAME: "Quick" or "Haste"

DATE: 10th Century BC

IDENTIFICATION: Friend and counselor to David who became a spy for him

STORY LINE: Hushai pretended to be loyal to Absalom, but he informed David

READ IT IN THE BIBLE: 2 Samuel 15:1–15, 30–37

mean more to you and to your kids than anything I could have gotten out of it."

Doing the right thing means not always doing the easy thing. Doing the best thing means not always doing the comfortable thing. Hushai certainly understood that.

Hushai the Archite was a friend and wise counselor

of King David. When David's son Absalom revolted against his father, David had to flee from Jerusalem. At first, Hushai accompanied David, but when news came that Ahithophel, David's other adviser, had switched loyalties and was siding with Absalom, David asked Hushai to do something difficult and dangerous. He instructed Hushai to return to the city, feign loyalty to his rebellious son, and act as a secret agent to the king. Hushai preferred to remain with David, but he knew that sometimes doing the right thing means doing the uncomfortable thing. Hushai provided reliable intelligence on the plans of Absalom and counseled the son in ways that benefited the father.

Sometimes God prompts us to do things we would prefer not to do. It might mean befriending an unfriendly neighbor or mentoring a teenager who has no positive influence in his or her life. For you, this may not always be the comfortable thing, but it's the right thing. Be responsive to God's promptings. Invade Satan's camp to serve your King and enjoy being God's secret agent.

ICHABOD

No God, No Glory

When I was a boy a stray dog wandered onto our farm. He was scrawny and looked like he had come out on the short end of many dog fights. We decided to keep him even though he was what you might

NAME: "Inglorious" or "No Glory"
DATE: 11th Century BC
IDENTIFICATION: Son of Phinehas, born when the Philistines captured the ark
STORY LINE: Mother named him in despair over news of the ark
READ IT IN THE BIBLE: 1 Samuel 4:1–22

picture Satan's dog to look like. His hair was jet black and shiny. We called him Ichabod.

The son of Phinehas and grandson of Eli the priest was the only man in the Bible named Ichabod. The Philistines were always a formidable enemy of Israel. When the Jews fought them at Aphek, Israel decided to take the ark of the covenant with them. If they thought that would bring them luck, it didn't.

While Eli sat waiting for a battle report, a runner hurried to him crying, "'your two sons, Hophni and Phineas, are dead; and the ark of God has been captured'" (1 Samuel 4:17). The ninety–eight–year–old priest was so distraught at all this bad news that he fell over backwards and broke his neck.

Hearing of these multiple tragedies, the widow of Phinehas went into labor and gave birth to a son, calling him Ichabod, which means "the glory of the Lord has departed." The widow knew that when God goes, the glory goes, too.

That's an important message for Christians and the Church in the 21st century. It doesn't matter how big your budget is or how many people attend the weekend services, when God goes, the glory goes. Pray for your church, your pastor, and yourself that no one will ever be able to call you Ichabod.

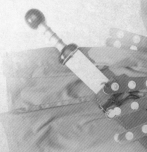

ISAAC

Personal Faith

I have always said that the best thing in the world is to be the father of a famous son, and the worst thing in the world is to be the son of a famous father. Isaac knew the best and the worst.

NAME: "Laughter"

DATE: 20th Century BC

IDENTIFICATION: Only son of Abraham by wife Sarah; second of the patriarchs

STORY LINE: Isaac lived between a powerful father and powerful son

READ IT IN THE BIBLE: Genesis 17:1–19; 32:22–30

Isaac's father, Abraham, was the first patriarch, the friend of God. God changed his name from Abram ("exalted father") to Abraham ("father of a multitude"). Isaac's son, Jacob, was also a great patriarch, the man from whom came the twelve tribes of Israel. God changed his name, too, from Jacob ("the supplanter") to Israel ("prince with God"). Nobody changed Isaac's name; he kept the same one for 180 years.

Isaac's mother thought it was a joke when she heard she was going to have a son in her old age, so he was named "laughter." But Isaac grew to be a man of faith in his own right.

Isaac demonstrated faith when Abraham took him to Mt. Moriah to sacrifice him. He had faith that the promises of God made to his father were made to him as well. In fact, Isaac's faith is mentioned often in the New Testament (see Acts 7:8; Romans 9:7; Galatians 4:21–31; and Hebrews 11:9–20). But the most important thing about Isaac's faith was that it was his own.

The faith of your father won't save you, and the faith of your son won't change your life.

Don't rely on someone's faith for your needs. "For by grace you have been saved through [your] faith . . . it is the gift of God; not of works, lest anyone should boast" (Ephesians 2:8–9). Make sure yours is a personal faith.

ISAIAH

Right–on Prophecies

Nostradamus. Hopi Prophecy. Edgar Cayce. The
Celestine Prophecies. White Buffalo. Mormon "White
Horse." New Age. Jeanne Dixon. Prophets come and
prophets go; some occasionally hit the nail on the
head. That was Isaiah.

NAME: "Jehovah is Salvation"
DATE: 8th Century BC
IDENTIFICATION: Son of Amoz, relative of the royal family,
famous prophet
STORY LINE: Prophesied Messiah's virgin birth and suffering death
READ IT IN THE BIBLE: Isaiah 7:1–14; 9:6; 53:1–12

In the year that King Uzziah died, God revealed
himself to the son of Amoz. Growing up in Jerusalem
afforded him the best education possible in the 8th
century BC. Isaiah's wife also was a prophetess. They
had two sons with the unlikely names of Shear–jashub
(Isaiah 7:3) and Maher–shalal–hash–baz (Isaiah 8:3).
Three of the greatest messianic prophecies of the

Old Testament came through the ministry of Isaiah. He recorded, "Behold, the virgin shall conceive and bear a Son, and shall call His name Immanuel" (7:14). Later Isaiah wrote, "For unto us a Child is born, unto us a Son is given; and the government will be upon His shoulder. And His name will be called Wonderful, Counselor, Mighty God, Everlasting Father, Prince of Peace. Of the increase of His government and peace there will be no end, upon the throne of David and over His kingdom . . . from that time forward, even forever . . ." (9:6,7). Near the end of the prophetic book that bears his name, Isaiah filled an entire chapter (53) with right–on references to Jesus as the Suffering Servant and Messiah.

Isaiah was a Jewish prophet writing about the Jewish Messiah. Take some time today to pray that the Jewish people will read their most famous prophet with open minds and that God will enable them to see that Messiah suffered and died for them at a place called Calvary.

ITTAI

An Unlikely Alliance

The Lone Ranger had Tonto, an unlikely companion. Sherlock Holmes had Watson, a complete mismatch. David had Ittai the Gittite, one of the most unlikely friendships ever.

NAME: "Timely"
DATE: 10th Century BC
IDENTIFICATION: Man from Gath who accompanied David in flight
STORY LINE: Ittai came to Jerusalem as Absalom drove David out
READ IT IN THE BIBLE: 2 Samuel 15:13–22; 18:1–5

Goliath of Gath was no match for the shepherd boy and his sling, but when David became king, he had more giant–sized problems to deal with. At one point, David's son Absalom rebelled against his father, and David had to flee from Jerusalem. Among those who fled with him was Ittai the Gittite.

When David saw that Ittai was in his entourage he suggested the Gittite return to Jerusalem. No one would blame him if he did. Ittai wasn't Jewish. He wasn't a member of the king's household. Besides, he had only arrived in Jerusalem the day before Absalom's rebellion. What horrible timing.

But Ittai refused, saying that he wanted to go wherever David went. The reason this alliance is so unlikely is that Ittai was a Gittite. Do you know what you call natives of the city of Gath, where Goliath lived? You guessed it. Gittites. After the rebellion was thwarted, David made Ittai commander over one third of his armies.

This is one of the most unlikely alliances in history. Still, it shows that it doesn't matter who you are, what your nationality or ethnic background is, if you want to enjoy the blessing of God, you need to hang out with the people of God.

Enjoy the fellowship of those whose skin color is different from yours or whose denomination is different from yours. You may just discover that one of your most faithful friends will also be one of your most unlikely friends.

JACOB

Back to Bethel

When John Wesley attended a Moravian meeting on Aldersgate Street in London, something amazing happened. The May 24, 1738, entry of his diary reads, "I felt my heart strangely warmed." The

NAME: "Supplanter"

DATE: 20th Century BC

IDENTIFICATION: Second of twins born to Isaac and Rebekah, father of Israel

STORY LINE: He had spiritual ups and downs, but always returned to God

READ IT IN THE BIBLE: Genesis 25:21–28; 28:10–22; 35:1–10

spiritual exchange that night between God and John Wesley changed the face of Christendom.

Long before Wesley, however, another life-changing encounter with God occurred for Jacob, one of the twin sons of Isaac and Rebekah. His life was filled with intrigue and deceit. Because he stole his brother's birthright, Jacob had to flee the Promised Land for Haran. But on his way "out of town," one of the most dramatic moments in Jacob's life occurred at Bethel (Genesis 28:10–22), when in his "Jacob's ladder" dream he received God's assurance, "Behold, I am with you and will keep you wherever you go, and will bring you back to this land." Jacob awoke and said, "Surely the Lord is in this place." He had met God in a personal way, just like John Wesley did.

Twenty years later God told Jacob to go back to Bethel (Genesis 35:1). Go back to the place where Jacob had driven down some spiritual stakes. Go back to where he could regain his intimacy with God, and he did.

Do you have a Bethel, a place where you remember your heart being strangely warmed toward God? Has that warmth cooled over the years? If you're not as intimate with God as you would like to be, if you're not as close to Him as you used to be, isn't it time you go back to your Bethel? Apply the 1 John 1:9 principle— "If we confess our sins, He is faithful and just to forgive us our sins"—to your life, and feel the warmth of God again.

JAEL

Action First, Applause Later

Pfc. Jessica Lynch was virtually unknown outside of her home town of Palestine, West Virginia, until the Iraq War. But when this 19 year–old soldier was caught in an ambush, endured broken bones, gunshot

NAME: "Mountain Goat"
DATE: 13th Century BC
IDENTIFICATION: Wife of Heber, Jael demonstrated her loyalty to Israel
STORY LINE: Jael drove a tent peg through the temple of Sisera
READ IT IN THE BIBLE: Judges 4:1–24

and stab wounds, and then was rescued by U.S. soldiers, this country girl became a national hero.

The Bible has its share of Jessica Lynch stories. It's filled with gripping accounts of obscure people who rose to meet challenges when they needed to. One of those obscure people is Jael, a homemaker in Israel.

Jael was the wife of Heber the Kenite, a descendant of Moses' father–in–law. Historically the

Kenite tribe had been long–standing allies of Israel. However, Jael's husband, for whatever reason, chose to side with the Canaanite king, Jabin, in his struggle against Israel. But Jael demonstrated her loyalty to Jehovah in one of those unique history–making events. She invited Sisera, Jabin's general, into her tent where she gave him milk to drink instead of water. That made him sleepy. While Sisera snoozed, Jael drove a tent peg through his temple into the ground. God subdued the Canaanites using a single act of bravery by an obscure housewife.

Do you feel too obscure, too distant from the podium, too far from the spotlight to be used by God? If so, learn from Jael. She didn't leave the spotlight to perform an act of bravery; she acted and then stepped into the spotlight. It's action first, applause later. Do whatever it is God has for you to do, and He'll take care of the applause.

JAHAZIEL

Encouragement

Have you ever been in a hole so deep only God could get you out? What did you do? If you're normal, you probably exhausted all your energy and resources trying to solve your problem before you asked God for help. Am I right?

NAME: "The Vision of God"
DATE: 9th Century BC
IDENTIFICATION: Levite of the sons of Asaph who encouraged Jehoshaphat
STORY LINE: He told Jehoshaphat to fight the Moabites and Ammonites
READ IT IN THE BIBLE: 2 Chronicles 20:1–17

King Jehoshaphat of Judah faced a challenge like that. A coalition of forces from east of the Dead Sea teamed up to threaten Jerusalem. When the king got the word, they had crossed the Jordan and were at En–gedi about to slice their way up the narrow canyons to Jerusalem. Jehoshaphat called for a fast and prayed to God, expressing his complete dependence on Jehovah for victory.

Suddenly the Spirit of God moved upon a Levite named Jahaziel to give encouragement to the king. "Do not be afraid nor dismayed because of this great multitude, for the battle is not yours, but God's" (2 Chronicles 20:15). In fact, God told Jahaziel that Judah's armies would not even have to fight the coalition troops. Instead they were simply to take their battle positions, stand still, and watch God work for them.

So encouraged was King Jehoshaphat that he sent the choir ahead of the army to sing praises to God for their impending victory. So confused were the Ammonites, Edomites, and Moabites that they turned on each other and completely slaughtered their own coalition forces.

It's amazing what a little encouragement can do. Could someone in your family, your church, your community or your office use some encouragement today? Remember, the battle is the Lord's. Don't make promises that cannot be kept, but remind others of the exceeding great and precious promises of God. Nothing will encourage them more.

JAMES

Staying at Home

I grew up in the rolling hills of western Pennsylvania. Nearby lived a simple, godly family named Hershey with five children. One by one they left home to go to the mission field. All but one, who stayed home to serve the Lord.

NAME: "Supplanter" ("Jacob" in Hebrew)
DATE: 1st Century AD
IDENTIFICATION: Oldest son of Mary and Joseph, author of the Book of James
STORY LINE: James was the oldest of Jesus' four younger brothers
READ IT IN THE BIBLE: Matthew 13:53–58; Acts 15:1–21

Not all of God's servants are called to leave home in answer to God's call. When Isaiah said, "Here am I! Send me," God sent him to his own people in his own land (Isaiah 6:8–9). And when the demoniac of Gadara wanted to go with Jesus after the Savior healed him, Christ told him to go home and tell his friends what the Lord had done for him (Mark 5:19).

While Thomas was going to India, Philip to Asia Minor, and Paul to the rest of the Roman world, someone had to remain behind in Jerusalem to faithfully lead the flock there. That someone was James, the younger brother of the Lord Jesus.

Like the rest of Jesus' brothers, James did not come to faith in Jesus until after His crucifixion. But in the Book of Acts James emerged as a leader of the Jerusalem church. His younger brothers also became believers and traveled to foreign places (1 Corinthians 9:5), but James knew the home front was his mission field (Galatians 2:9).

If you long for a passport filled with stamps from foreign countries, but instead you just have a class of junior high boys, be encouraged by James. It was his junior high boys who were the next generation of those sent out to capture the world for Christ. Your home job is important. Be proud of it.

JASHOBEAM

Loyalty and Bravery

Lt. Col. Stephen Twitty was awarded the Silver Star, the third highest medal in the U.S. Army, for leading the spearhead attack into the City of Baghdad during the Iraq War. Lt. Col. Twitty led one thousand men into battle and lost only two, with thirty other soldiers

NAME: "Captivity of the People"
DATE: 10th Century BC
IDENTIFICATION: A Hacmonite, son of Zabdiel, captain of David's mighty men
STORY LINE: Jashobeam killed 300 men in one bloody battle
READ IT IN THE BIBLE: 1 Chronicles 11:1–14; 27:1–2

wounded. Twitty said he had to go off on his own and meditate and pray for God to keep him focused so he could keep his soldiers focused.

Every generation has its heroes. None stand taller in David's army than Jashobeam. The son of Zabdiel, a Hacmonite, Jashobeam became famous for an unbelievable victory in which he killed three hundred soldiers at one time. But Jashobeam was as mighty in loyalty as he was mighty in battle.

Once when the Philistines had bogged David down in the cave of Adullam, David mused to himself, "Oh, that someone would give me a drink of the water from the well of Bethlehem, which is by the gate!" Jashobeam overheard David and with two other "mighty men" fought his way through enemy lines to the Bethlehem well and retrieved a drink for David. They then fought their way back to Adullam and presented the cool water to David, who immediately poured it out on the ground as a sacrifice to God in honor of their bravery (2 Samuel 23:13–17).

God is looking for heroes in the battle against Satan. All a hero needs is to fight bravely and prove his loyalty to our Commander–in–Chief. Is there some battle for righteousness you could join today? Are you ready to be one of God's heroes? Ask God to help keep you focused.

JEHOASH

Good Economy, Bad Morality

"It was the best of times; it was the worst of times."
Not just a line from *The Tale of Two Cities,* that's an
apt description of society today. Never before have we
had such expensive homes with so many gadgets as we

NAME: "Fire of Jehovah"
DATE: 8th Century BC
IDENTIFICATION: 13th king of Northern Kingdom; son (Joash) of
   Jehoahaz
STORY LINE: Jehoash was a political success, but was spiritually
   bankrupt
READ IT IN THE BIBLE: 2 Kings 13:10–16; 22–25

do today. Yet with all the advances in technology, our
postmodern world is morally bankrupt.

This is not the first time the economy was good
and the morality was bad. In the days of Jehoash, also
called Joash, prosperity abounded. Israel had been
through some tough times under Jehoash's father,
Jehoahaz, and his grandfather, Jehu, but now things
were looking up. The borders were quiet after many

years of intimidation by the Syrians. The gross national product steadily improved during the sixteen years Jehoash reigned in Samaria. But Jehoash did evil in the sight of the Lord.

Economic good times often coincide with moral bad times. During the decade of the 90s the stock market soared. There were profits aplenty in every portfolio. But greed dominated many corporate headquarters, and corporate scandals abounded as the economy retreated. The White House, too, was scandalized as the country was embarrassed by presidential moral indiscretions.

It doesn't have to be this way, of course. The Bible promises, "Blessed is the nation whose God is the LORD" (Psalm 33:12). Blessing comes in many forms—financial, physical, spiritual, moral, and the like—but national blessing only comes when the people desire righteousness more than they desire prosperity.

Do as the apostle Paul suggests. Take some time today to pray for your nation and your leaders (1 Timothy 2:1–2). A good economy is nowhere near the blessing of good morality.

Blessed

is the nation
whose God
is the LORD.

—Psalm 33:12

JEHOIACHIN

The Coniah Curse

If you've ever doubted God's ability to accomplish His purpose, even in the midst of adverse circumstances, doubt no more. The Coniah curse is proof positive that God is in control.

NAME: "Jehovah Establishes"
DATE: 6th Century BC
IDENTIFICATION: 19th king of Southern Kingdom; son (Coniah) of Jehoiakim
STORY LINE: Jehoiachin's descendants were banned from David's throne
READ IT IN THE BIBLE: 2 Kings 24:1–20; Jeremiah 22:24–30

Jehoiachin became Judah's king just three months before Nebuchadnezzar captured Jerusalem. Also known as Jeconiah or Coniah, Jehoiachin was so wicked that God cursed him and all of his offspring. Recorded in Jeremiah 22, the Coniah curse concludes with, "Write this man down as childless, a man who shall not prosper in his days; for none of his descendants shall prosper, sitting on the throne of

David, and ruling anymore in Judah" (v. 30).

What makes this curse troublesome is that it's placed on the line of Christ's ancestors. No one born of Jeconiah would ever prosper on the throne of David, and yet this is the only line through which the Messiah and King can legally come. That's a problem!

But God is in control. Matthew 1 presents the genealogy of David through Solomon, and includes Joseph, the husband of Mary. While Jesus was Joseph's legal son and thus heir to David's throne, He was not his biological son. Jesus is biologically connected to David through his son Nathan (Luke 3:31), in whose line Mary was born. As a result of His legal connection to David through Joseph and His biological connection through Mary, Jesus avoided the Coniah curse and is the only person who can legitimately rule on David's throne with God's blessing.

Take some time today to thank God for being God. Only an omniscient Sovereign like Jehovah could guide the events of history so that Jesus is alone qualified to be the Messiah and Savior of the world.

JEREMIAH

Politically Incorrect

When President George W. Bush signed into law a ban on partial–birth abortion, he vowed to "vigorously defend this law against any who would try to challenge it in the court." He knew the law would

NAME: "Jehovah Lifts Up"

DATE: 7th Century BC

IDENTIFICATION: The "weeping" prophet from the village of Anathoth

STORY LINE: Jeremiah predicted God would use Babylon to punish Judah

Read it in the Bible: Jeremiah 25:1–14

offend some Americans, but he chose to stand on his principles rather than cave to political pressure.

In the Bible, the prophet Jeremiah did the same. He is the quintessential example of someone who preferred truth to popularity.

Born in the village of Anathoth, north of Jerusalem, God sanctioned Jeremiah as a prophet even before he was born (Jeremiah 1:5). Jeremiah was

God's major mouthpiece during the decline and fall of the southern kingdom. He spoke for God during the reigns of Judah's last five kings.

Jeremiah is often called "the weeping prophet" because he wept openly over the sins of his nation. Though it was both unpopular and politically incorrect, he predicted God would not spare the Jews from Nebuchadnezzar, but that God would use Babylon to carry off the Israelites into captivity as punishment for their sins. Obviously that didn't go over very well with the Jews, who branded Jeremiah a traitor and a subversive. Just as he predicted, however, in 587 BC Jerusalem was destroyed and most of her people were deported to Babylon. Jeremiah remained in Jerusalem living under the authority of a ruling governor appointed by Babylon, but eventually he was forced to flee to Egypt for safety.

Often the right message isn't the popular message. Jeremiah had to choose between being faithful in delivering God's truth or being politically correct. You and I face that same decision daily. Choose carefully. Popularity lasts but a moment; truth lasts forever.

JEROBOAM 1

Being Remembered

Swiss amateur–mountaineer George de Mestral is best remembered for inventing Velcro. Neal Armstrong is the astronaut who took "one small step for man, one giant leap for mankind." Michael Jordan is remembered for his ability to become airborne on his

NAME: "He Who Opposes the People"
DATE: 10th Century BC
IDENTIFICATION: 1st king of Northern Kingdom; son of Nebat
STORY LINE: Jeroboam built alternate worship centers at Dan and Bethel
READ IT IN THE BIBLE: 1 Kings 12:1–33

way to the basket. And Frank Zamboni will go down in history as the man who developed the ice resurfacing machine he named after himself.

What do you want to be remembered for? Every time someone mentions your name, what next do you want to come out of their mouth? That was a problem for Jeroboam.

After the death of King Solomon, Jeroboam, the son of Nebat from Ephraim's tribe, asked Rehoboam, who ruled in his father's place, to ease the tax burden on the people. The wise elders told Rehoboam to lighten the taxes; his younger, hot-headed friends told him to increase them. When the people's taxes did increase, Jeroboam led a rebellion of the ten northern tribes and seceded from the Hebrew Union.

Anxious to solidify his hold on the Northern Kingdom, and fearful that if his countrymen traveled to Jerusalem to worship they would revert to the Davidic kingdom, Jeroboam built centers of worship in Bethel and Dan as alternative sites and instituted the idolatrous practice of worshipping a golden calf. It was this that caused him thereafter to be called "Jeroboam, the son of Nebat, who made Israel sin" (1 Kings 22:52; 2 Kings 3:3, 10:29, 13:2, 13:11, 14:24, 15:9, 15:18, 15:24, 15:28, 23:15).

Often our relationship with God determines what we are remembered for. Do those things that please God today. You can be like Abraham, the friend of God, or like Jeroboam, the man who made Israel sin. Choose wisely; choose well.

JESUS

The Most Unique Person in the World

Michael Hart wrote a book entitled *The 100: A Ranking of the Most Influential Persons in History*. Most people wouldn't have the nerve to suggest the one hundred most influential people of all time, and even fewer would dare to rank them one to one hundred.

NAME: "Savior"
DATE: 1st Century AD
IDENTIFICATION: Descendant of David, Son of God, Savior of the world
STORY LINE: Jesus came to die to pay the penalty for our sin
READ IT IN THE BIBLE: John 3:1–18

It will not surprise you that Jesus Christ is in that list. What may surprise you is where He was ranked. Michael Hart placed Jesus third, behind Mohammed and Sir Isaac Newton. Buddha and Confucius came next. Obviously Michael Hart has never met Jesus Christ for there is nobody like Him.

Jesus' birth was absolutely unique. He was born of a virgin, born the God–man, 100 percent God and 100 percent man. Mohammed could not make that claim. Jesus' death was also unique, not because He was crucified, but because Jesus died as our substitute, paying the penalty for our sin. Isaac Newton couldn't have done that.

Jesus' resurrection was also unique. Others died and were raised to life, but they all died again. Jesus was raised to live forever and was exalted at the right hand of God the Father. There is just no one like Jesus, "Nor is there salvation in any other, for there is no other name under heaven given among men by which we must be saved" (Acts 4:12).

This world may have many religions, but it still has only one Savior. In case you haven't done it yet, take some time right now to thank God for giving us His greatest gift. "For God so loved the world that He gave His only begotten Son, that whoever believes in Him should not perish but have everlasting life" (John 3:16).

JOAB

Jekyll and Hyde

The life of Joab could have been the basis for Robert Lewis Stevenson's *The Strange Case of Dr. Jekyll and Mr. Hyde.* One minute Joab was a hero, the next he was a scoundrel.

NAME: "Jehovah is Father"
DATE: 10th Century BC
IDENTIFICATION: One of three sons of Zeruiah, David's sister; David's general
STORY LINE: Joab lived by the sword and died by the sword
READ IT IN THE BIBLE: 1 Chronicles 11:1–9; 2 Samuel 10:6–16; 1 Kings 2:28–35

Joab, Abishai, and Asahel were the sons of Zeruiah, David's sister. Joab rose to prominence at the battle of Gibeon when Saul's troops under Abner were vanquished. Later he distinguished himself by attacking the Jebusite stronghold on Mount Zion by climbing up into the city through a water shaft. David made his nephew general of his armies.

But for all his military valor and incredible loyalty

142

to David, Joab had a mean streak. He could morph from Dr. Jekyll to Mr. Hyde in no time. Because Abner had slain Joab's brother Asahel, Joab killed Abner in revenge. Joab failed to question David's command to place Uriah the Hittite in the heat of the battle so he would die, thus covering David's sin with Bathsheba.

When Absalom, Joab's cousin, rebelled against his father, David, Joab ignored a direct order from David and brutally killed Absalom. This insubordination led David to replace Joab as commander with another of Joab's cousins, Amasa. Enraged by jealous hate, Joab killed Amasa. When David's son Adonijah moved to become the king, Joab sided with him against Solomon, and he was killed by Benaiah when he fled into the tabernacle.

Joab was a military hero, but he couldn't control his jealousy and anger. Nothing will destroy you more quickly. Learn from Joab's Jekyll and Hyde life. Guard your integrity. Be a person of honor and decency all the time.

JOB

God's Restraining Power

If you have become victim to waves of misfortune, perhaps you can identify with Job. For him, it was like constantly stepping on the teeth of a garden rake. Wham! Right in the face.

NAME: "Foe" or "Persecuted"
DATE: Unknown; early BC
IDENTIFICATION: A wealthy businessman from Uz, greatest man in his day
STORY LINE: God permitted multiple disasters to prove Job's character
READ IT IN THE BIBLE: Job 1:1–22

Job was a man of great wealth, respect, and personal property. In fact, he was one of the richest sheiks of antiquity. He was also blameless and upright, a man of impeccable integrity. When Satan contended that Job only feared God because God had been so good to him, Jehovah permitted Satan to take all that Job had, except for Job's life. Satan was powerless to do more than God allowed.

Another way to understand this is in the story of a boy who was fascinated with the neighborhood blacksmith. He spent hours watching the smithy work. The blacksmith would take a red–hot piece of iron out of the furnace, place it on the anvil, and tap it with a tiny hammer. Then his big bruiser of an assistant would strike a mighty blow in the same spot with a heavy sledge hammer. Once the boy commented to the blacksmith, "You don't do much good with that little hammer, do you?" The man replied, "Oh, but I do. I show that big guy where to hit."

Do you feel that Satan is using his heaviest hammer on you? Take heart! Satan can do nothing to you beyond the permission of God. God is like that blacksmith. He shows Satan where he can hit, but God will never allow him to strike a blow that will break you. He is too kind and gracious for that.

Express your confidence in God's restraining power, and encourage those around you today.

JOHN

Caring for the Elderly

Did you know that nearly one out of every four U.S. households provides care to a relative or friend aged 50 or older? About 15 percent of U.S. adults care for a seriously ill or disabled family member. And about 7.3 million people are informal caregivers, such as

NAME: "Jehovah is Gracious"
DATE: 1st Century AD
IDENTIFICATION: Son of Zebedee and Salome, closest disciple to Jesus
STORY LINE: At His crucifixion, Jesus committed His mother's care to John
READ IT IN THE BIBLE: John 19:17–27

spouses, family, or neighbors. Having someone committed into your care is a big responsibility. No one in the Bible knew that better than Jesus' close friend John.

John was a fisherman on the Sea of Galilee. It was a family business. His brother James and father, Zebedee, were also fishermen. John served Jesus faithfully during his life. He was such a close disciple of the Lord that when Jesus hung on Calvary's cross, He called out to John and His mother at the foot of the cross. To His mother He said, "Woman, behold your son!" And to John He said, "Behold your mother" (John 19:26–27). Jesus was committing the care of His mother to His most trusted friend.

Tradition says that John settled in Ephesus and Mary went with him. During Domitian's reign over the Roman Empire, AD 81–96, John was banished to the isle of Patmos where he received the Revelation, but throughout his ministry he cared for Mary as he had promised his Savior.

Do you have someone you need to care for today? Maybe they are in an assisted living or a long–term care facility, but you are responsible for their care. Be honored. There is no greater trust than the trust an older person places in the one who cares for them. Treat them as a treasure. They are!

JOHN THE BAPTIST

Fading into the Background

Remember the 286 personal computer? It was light years ahead of the typewriter, but when the Pentium came along it blinked into computer history.

It would not be easy for John the Baptist to fade into the background, but he did. God's angel said of

NAME: "Jehovah is Gracious"
DATE: 1st Century AD
IDENTIFICATION: Son of Zechariah and Elizabeth, forerunner of the Messiah
STORY LINE: John pointed to Jesus and chose to decrease in stature
READ IT IN THE BIBLE: John 1:19–29; 3:23–36

him: "He will be great in the sight of the Lord . . . He will also be filled with the Holy Spirit, even from his mother's womb" (Luke 1:15). Jesus testified that "among those born of women there is not a greater prophet than John the Baptist" (Luke 7:28).

Still, for all the accolades, John knew he was just a forerunner. He claimed, "I am 'the voice of one crying in the wilderness'" (John 1:23), and so he was. John was raised in the wilderness, called by God there, preached there, and probably killed at Herod's fortress there. John's ministry was one of preparation; he paved the way for Jesus. He knew he was not worthy even to loosen the sandals of the One coming after him. When John saw Jesus he proclaimed, "Behold! The Lamb of God who takes away the sin of the world!" (John 1:29).

John knew he had to decrease so Jesus' reputation could increase. That's the way it is with you and me. If we want the world to see Jesus, we must fade into the background. We must talk of our Savior and not of ourselves. We must promote His agenda and not our own.

Ask yourself today how you're doing at pointing others toward the Savior. Then ask God to help you fade to the background so the world can see Jesus.

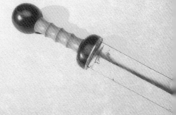

JONAH

A Second Chance

God is the God of the second chance. If you've muffed your life, the God of the Bible is the God for you.

The prophet Jonah needed a second chance. God charged him to go to Nineveh and cry out against the wickedness of that great city. But Nineveh belonged to

NAME: "Dove"
DATE: 8th Century BC
IDENTIFICATION: Son of Amittai of Gath–hepher, prophet, fish bait, missionary
STORY LINE: When Jonah disobeyed, God gave him a second chance
READ IT IN THE BIBLE: Jonah 1:1–17; 3:1–10

the Assyrians, the bitter enemies of the Jews. *How could God be serious?,* Jonah must have wondered. So the prophet went instead to Joppa and boarded a ship bound for the West.

When a storm arose and Jonah was tossed into the sea, God already had prepared a great fish to swallow Jonah—not to punish him, but to save his life. The fish coughed Jonah up on dry land, and Jonah 3:1 says, "Now the word of the LORD came to Jonah the second time." God gave this disobedient prophet a second chance.

And Jonah's not alone. John Mark blew his first missionary assignment, but God gave him a second chance. Peter denied his Lord three times, but God gave him a second chance.

One of the most tender verses in the Bible is Jeremiah 18:4. The potter was making something on his wheel, but the vessel was marred in the potter's hand. "So he made it again into another vessel . . . ." A second chance.

Do you need a second chance today? Has your life been one disappointment after another? Be encouraged. God is the God of a second chance. Confess any known sin to Him, forsake it, and ask Him to help you start over. He will, you know; He's just that kind of God.

JOSEPH

Good from Evil

The United States has seen its share of disasters. On September 8, 1900, an estimated 6,000–8,000 people died in Galveston, Texas, as a result of a tidal surge caused by a hurricane. In Chicago, May 25, 1979, an American Airlines DC–10 crashed seconds after

NAME: "Jehovah Will Add"
DATE: 19th Century BC
IDENTIFICATION: Favorite son of Jacob, became Prime Minister of Egypt
STORY LINE: Jealous brothers were used of God to save their family
READ IT IN THE BIBLE: Genesis 37:1–36; 50:15–21

takeoff, killing all 272 people aboard and three on the ground. But no disaster in U.S. history can compare to September 11, 2001. In the terrorist attacks of that dreadful day, 2,995 people lost their lives.

Such disasters frequently prompt us to ask, "How could a good God allow these things to happen?" That's what Joseph may have wanted to know, except he already knew the answer.

Joseph was his father's favorite child, and his brothers hated him for it. They sold him to a Midianite caravan going to Egypt and told their father he was dead. In that foreign land Joseph was falsely accused, imprisoned, and completely forgotten— by everyone but God. But his faith in God was rewarded; Joseph was elevated to a position second only to Pharaoh. When the disaster of famine in Canaan drove his brothers to seek help in Egypt, they bowed before the brother they had hated.

Eventually Joseph's whole family moved to Egypt. The disasters of Joseph's life were turned into something beautiful by God. Joseph said to his brothers, "You meant evil against me; but God meant it for good."

Disasters defy explanation, but so does God. The pain of disaster is real, but so is God's grace. If you're facing dark days in your life, don't blame God. He didn't cause your problems, but He can make something good out of them, if you trust Him.

JOSEPH OF ARIMATHEA

Boldness

New Yorkers always appreciated their police officers
and firemen, but most people didn't really think of
them as heroes. Then terrorists flew hijacked airplanes
into the Twin Towers, and on September 11, 2001,
Big Apple perceptions changed forever.

NAME: "Jehovah Will Add"
DATE: 1st Century AD
IDENTIFICATION: Rich man, member of the Sanhedrin, buried
   Jesus' body
STORY LINE: A secret disciple of Jesus; crucifixion brought boldness
READ IT IN THE BIBLE: Luke 23:26–56

Often a single event defines our lives. That's the
way it was for Joseph, a wealthy man from Arimathea,
northwest of Jerusalem. His life had been shaped by
his religion. He was a righteous man who eagerly
anticipated the kingdom of God. His religious life
contributed to him being selected to join the
Sanhedrin, the religious court of Judaism. But it also

contributed to an emptiness and a longing for intimacy with God that religion could not satisfy.

Somehow and somewhere Joseph of Arimathea encountered Jesus of Nazareth, and he found in the Savior all he did not find in the rituals of his religion. He kept his discipleship a secret for fear of what his fellow Jews would say. Then came the crucifixion. That single event changed Joseph's life forever. No longer could he be quiet. He didn't care what his fellow Sanhedrinists would say. After the crucifixion, Joseph boldly secured permission from Pilate to take the body of Jesus from Calvary and to place it in his own family tomb nearby. His love for the Lord Jesus would be a secret no longer.

Is your love for Jesus a secret? Do your friends and family know you are a Christ–follower? If not, ask God to make you bold in your witness today and enjoy the privilege of identifying with Jesus Christ, the only Savior this world will ever have.

JOSEPH

Do the Right Thing, in the Right Way

Of all the characters in the biblical account of Jesus' birth, I feel most sorry for Joseph. A carpenter living in Nazareth, Joseph could trace his lineage to King David through Solomon. Still, he was a humble man

NAME: "Jehovah Will Add"
DATE: 1st Century AD
IDENTIFICATION: Husband of Mary, the mother of Jesus; Nazareth carpenter
STORY LINE: When Mary became pregnant, Joseph did the right thing
READ IT IN THE BIBLE: Matthew 1:18–25

and desperately in love with Mary, who also was a humble woman and a virgin.

But something happened that shook Joseph to his very core. Mary was discovered to be pregnant, and Joseph was certain he wasn't the father. Being a righteous man, Joseph knew he had to break their betrothal and give Mary the required papers of divorce (Deuteronomy 24:1). But because he was an honorable man and loved her still, Joseph determined not to haul Mary before a magistrate but instead to file the papers in the presence of only two or three witnesses. He wanted to spare Mary as much shame as he could.

While contemplating his grim options, the angel of the Lord appeared to Joseph in a dream and assured him of Mary's love, purity, and faithfulness. The angel informed him that Mary had been faithful, that she had conceived by the Holy Spirit of God, and that her baby would be the Messiah of the Jews and the Savior of mankind.

Joseph is a stellar example of a man caught between two duties. His righteousness made him do the right thing, but his love drove him to do it with the least fanfare possible. If you are facing a difficult decision today, one that impacts friends or family, do the right thing, but do it in the right way. The more shame you spare others, the more of Christ's love you show them.

JOSHUA

Following God's Directions

When I buy Christmas presents, I try to avoid three little words—"Some Assembly Required." The directions never make sense to me, but I've discovered that if I follow them I get the job done right.

NAME: "Jehovah is Salvation"
DATE: 15th Century BC
IDENTIFICATION: Moses' successor who led Israel to conquer the Promised Land
STORY LINE: Joshua proved his faith when he obeyed what made no sense
READ IT IN THE BIBLE: Joshua 5:13–6:25

Joshua learned that at Jericho. Before the famous battle began, Joshua was out surveying the city, determining his battle plan. Suddenly, the Commander of the Lord's army appeared to Joshua with his sword drawn. This was a pre–incarnate appearance of Jesus Himself, and He was there to reveal the divine battle plan to Joshua. It was the craziest thing this battle–tested soldier had ever heard.

The Commander told Joshua to march around the city once each day for six days and then seven times on the seventh day. Then the priests would blow their trumpets, the people would shout, and the walls of the impregnable city of Jericho would fall down flat. I feel pretty certain Joshua questioned how this plan would work, but he never questioned the One who gave it to him. The people did exactly as the Lord commanded, and the results were exactly what He foretold.

Sometimes God asks us to do things we don't understand. There are instructions given in the Bible that don't always make sense to us. The key, however, is obedience, not understanding. It is not always necessary that we understand, but it is always necessary that we obey. Ask God to help you obey His Word today, even if you don't understand everything in it. That's the key to victory.

JOSIAH

Rediscovering God's Word

There it sits—imposing and largely unread. We all have one. But we don't read it, and our lack of familiarity with it has reduced our influence on society. I'm talking, of course, about the Bible. If

NAME: "Fire of Jehovah"
DATE: 7th Century BC
IDENTIFICATION: 16th king of Southern Kingdom; son of Amon
STORY LINE: Discovery of the Bible brings national, spiritual reform
READ IT IN THE BIBLE: 2 Chronicles 34:1–33

Christians all blew the dust off their Bibles at the same time, we'd suffocate in the dust storm.

To have a Bible and not read it is as devastating as not having one at all. Ask King Josiah. The three decades of his reign were the happiest years in Judah's history and for good reason.

Josiah was eight years old when he became king. By age 16 he began "to seek the God of his father

David" (2 Chronicles 34:3). When he was 20 Josiah became concerned over Judah's idolatry and launched a major offensive to eliminate it. At 26, he ordered Solomon's Temple to be cleansed and repaired, and in the process Hilkiah the priest found the Book of the Law. It had been neglected in the dust and debris of the temple, probably because Josiah's grandfather, Manasseh, attempted to eradicate its influence. But when God's Word was read to Josiah, the king was horrified to learn how far Judah had departed from God, and the pace of his reforms quickened.

If you believe society is sinking into the quagmire of immorality and idolatry, learn from Josiah's experience. Spiritual reform always begins with the rediscovery of God's Word. If the American church began to read the Bible they love, they might make a positive impact on the land they love. Let the spiritual reform begin with you. Read your Bible systematically, daily, completely, and become a change agent.

JUDAH

Taking Responsibility

When Patrick Reynolds signed on to help the
American Lung Association's anti–smoking campaign
it raised quite a few eyebrows. Why? Because Patrick
is the grandson of the founder of the R. J. Reynolds

NAME: "Praise"
DATE: 19th Century BC
IDENTIFICATION: 4th son of Jacob and Leah, he received Jacob's
    blessing
STORY LINE: Judah's line became the Messianic line of Christ
READ IT IN THE BIBLE: Genesis 49:1–12

Tobacco Company. His reason? "To make up for the
damage my family has done."

Taking personal responsibility for our actions—
or the actions of our family, our church or our
community—is never easy. Just ask Judah.

Seven men in the Old Testament answered to the
name Judah, but one stood head and shoulders above
the others. He was Jacob's son by Leah, founder of the

tribal family from which the Messiah would come.

Judah wasn't perfect, but he often assumed leadership in the patriarchal family even though he wasn't the oldest son. His behavior with his daughter–in–law Tamar showed some flaws in his character, but he came to grips with his sin and never returned to it (Genesis 38:26). When Jacob's sons journeyed to Egypt in search of grain, the Egyptian Prime Minister, who was their brother Joseph although they didn't know it, demanded that their youngest brother be brought to him. Judah took personal responsibility for Benjamin's safety. Perhaps it was this sense of personal responsibility that prompted Jacob to send Judah ahead of the family as point man when they moved to Egypt.

Taking personal responsibility is not something postmodern people do well. But one of the greatest signs of godly character is owning up to mistakes and taking leadership to make things right. If you need to take personal responsibility in something today, ask God to give you courage and do the right thing. Let Judah be your inspiration.

JUDE

Truth Drifters

Our hearts ache when we see friends and family ensnared by false teaching. That made Jude's heart ache, too, and precipitated his tiny epistle in the New Testament.

NAME: "Praise"
DATE: 1st Century AD
IDENTIFICATION: Brother of Jesus, disciple, author of the Book of Jude
STORY LINE: Jude showed concern for those who drift from the truth
READ IT IN THE BIBLE: Mark 6:1–6; Jude 1–25

Jude is an English form of the name Judas. He mentions his brother is James, and it is quite likely that both were the half–brothers of the Lord Jesus (Matthew 13:55). But neither of them believed in the Savior until after His resurrection (Acts 1:14). Jude could have established his credibility by claiming to be the Lord's brother; instead he claimed to be the Lord's bondservant (Jude 1).

This humble servant wanted to write to his friends about the joys of their common salvation, but instead he found it necessary to warn them to contend earnestly for the faith. Some of their friends and family had fallen into cults that denied the lordship of Jesus Christ. To deny Christ's lordship is to deny the Christian faith. That's why Jude urged them to engage those who had drifted from the truth in dialogue, in solid biblical teaching, and in their prayers.

Unfortunately, truth drifters are common in every generation of the faith. They hear a television preacher or listen to the false teaching of someone who appears at their door, and they are ensnared. If you have family or friends who have become truth drifters, don't avoid them, engage them. Talk with them about the faith that was once for all delivered to the saints. Help people to see that new teaching cannot compare to old truth. Pray for them and don't give up on them. God rescues truth drifters every day.

KETURAH

Second String

Runner–up. Second chair. Also ran. Never mind that you were ahead of all but one, nobody likes to be second.

Keturah learned how to play second fiddle, and she did it very well. Abraham loved his beautiful wife, Sarah. But the great patriarch also had another wife.

NAME: "Fragrance" or "Incense"
DATE: 22nd Century BC
IDENTIFICATION: Abraham's second wife, she bore six sons to the Patriarch
STORY LINE: Keturah brought love and companionship to Abraham's old age
READ IT IN THE BIBLE: Genesis 25:1–11

No, not Hagar, the mother of Ishmael. This was a later wife, a concubine, named Keturah. She was only a secondary wife until Sarah died, but in Abraham's old age, Keturah brought him companionship, not to mention six sons: Zimran, Jokshan, Medan, Midian, Ishbak, and Shuah.

Nobody likes to be second, but that doesn't have to

get us down. George Gershwin was the second-born son, but composed the incomparably beautiful "Rhapsody in Blue." John F. Kennedy was the second-born son, but became a popular American president. Most of the time when we are second we can't help it. We don't control everything, but we can control whether we allow being second fiddle to ruin our happiness, or whether we go ahead and play our hearts out.

Keturah's sons did not receive an inheritance from Abraham. Instead, he gave them gifts and sent them away. Did that stop them? Not at all. They founded six powerful tribes stretching from the Arabian Desert to the northern Euphrates. Their descendants were involved in international trade (Isaiah 60:6) as merchants (Genesis 37) and shepherds (Exodus 2:16). One of them, the queen of Sheba, came to visit King Solomon on an important trade mission (1 Kings 10:2). So whether it's second born, a second career or just second place, give it your best shot. Playing second fiddle is much better than not being in the orchestra.

LABAN

Cheating

When I was a teenager our high school math teacher bought the farm next to ours. He didn't know much about farming, but he knew a lot about dishonesty. He hired me to help him get his hay in one year, promising

NAME: "White"
DATE: 20th Century BC
IDENTIFICATION: Son of Bethuel, brother of Rebekah, father of Leah and Rachel
STORY LINE: Laban schemed to get more years of service from Jacob
READ IT IN THE BIBLE: Genesis 29:1–30

me a fair wage. But when the job was finished, he told me he had no money. I had been cheated.

Jacob must have felt the same way. When he fled to Haran to escape the hatred of his brother, Esau, he hired on with Laban, his uncle. His part—seven years of hard labor. The payback—the hand of Rachel, Laban's daughter, in marriage. Jacob was so in love with Rachel it seemed like a good deal.

But when it came time to pay up, Laban switched his older daughter, Leah, as Jacob's wife. Jacob was outraged. He had been cheated. He had to work another seven years for Rachel. In all, Jacob worked twenty years for Laban and finally decided he had had enough. He took his family and headed home to Canaan. But Laban soon overtook Jacob. After some words, Jacob and Laban erected a small heap of stones as mutual testimony they would never again have any dealings with each other. They repeated the Mizpeh benediction: "May the Lord watch between you and me when we are absent one from another" (Genesis 31:49). Usually a bond between friends, this became a pact between adversaries.

If your boss or brother–in–law or anybody else is cheating you today, ask God to give you strength to be honest with them, even if they aren't honest with you. After all, God keeps good payroll records.

May the Lord *watch* between you and me when we are absent one from another.

—Genesis 31:49

LAZARUS

Tragedy or Triumph?

She was young; just 17. In a horrible diving accident she snapped her neck and was left a quadriplegic. In the months that followed, Joni Eareckson Tada wrestled with the overwhelming impression that God had abandoned her. From her personal tragedy,

NAME: "God Has Helped"
DATE: 1st Century AD
IDENTIFICATION: The brother of Martha and Mary in Bethany, friend of Jesus
STORY LINE: Lazarus' resurrection proved God knows what He is doing
READ IT IN THE BIBLE: John 11:1–44

however, grew a personal relationship with God that changed her life and inspired a powerful ministry.

Different lenses. We often see things differently from God. You and I see a tragedy; God sees an opportunity. You and I see quicksand; God sees a launching pad. No person in the Bible better demonstrates the difference between divine eyes and our own eyes than Lazarus.

Life is filled with unexpected pain. But no pain equals the pain of death. Lazarus was Jesus' close friend, but even God's friends die. When Jesus heard that His friend had died, He delayed in returning to Bethany. Nobody understood why. God doesn't do things the way we do. When He finally arrived, both of Lazarus' sisters, Martha and Mary, took Jesus to task for not coming sooner. *Had He come, maybe Lazarus would not have died,* they thought. Jesus said to Martha, "Did I not say to you that if you would believe you would see the glory of God?" (John 11:40). Lazarus' sisters had death on their minds; Jesus had resurrection on His mind.

Sometimes what is dark and menacing to us is transformed into what is light and encouraging by Jesus. What was tragedy for Joni Eareckson Tada became triumph. In her accident she incurred genuine loss, but also discovered genuine purpose. She had a choice to focus on her loss or her purpose. She chose purpose. We all face the same choice.

LEAH

Ferrari and Zamboni

Remember the Smothers Brothers, Tom and Dick? They were the classic mismatch. Dick was smooth and sophisticated. Tommy stammered and stumbled through every conversation. He was famous for his line: "Mom always liked you best."

NAME: "Weary"
DATE: 20th Century BC
IDENTIFICATION: The older daughter of Laban, deceitfully married to Jacob
STORY LINE: Although less lovely than her sibling, Leah was a good wife
READ IT IN THE BIBLE: Genesis 29:1–35

Maybe you've thought people like others better than you. Perhaps you've even felt unloved by your own family. They're all Ferraris and you're a Zamboni. Everyone talks about your lovely size–four sister. Somehow words like "frumpy" creep into their vocabulary when they talk about you.

Leah was the older daughter of Laban, and she had

that problem, too. Her sister Rachel was beautiful. Their father's shepherds would crane their necks just to get a look at Rachel, while Leah, on the other hand, would walk by unnoticed. When Jacob came to Haran looking for a bride, who did he fall in love with? Rachel, of course.

And even when Laban pawned Leah off as wife on unsuspecting Jacob, he still loved Rachel more. But God has His way of making up for life's little inequities. He blessed Leah and Jacob with six sons and one daughter. That's half of the twelve tribes of Jacob. Rachel only bore Jacob two sons. It was Leah, not Rachel, who gave birth to Judah, through whose line Jesus the Messiah was eventually born.

If your sibling gets more attention than you do, take encouragement from Leah. Do all God gives you to do. Live the way that pleases Him the most, and let Him surprise you with life's little blessings the way He did Leah. After all, sometimes the one people notice least is the one God notices most.

LOIS

A Grandmother's Influence

Do you know the most influential position in the world? It's not the president of the United States. It's a grandma. Are you surprised?

Lois is the quintessential grandma of the Bible. She was the mother of Eunice and the grandmother

NAME: "Better" or "More Desirable"

DATE: 1st Century AD

IDENTIFICATION: Devout Jewess, mother of Eunice, grandmother of Timothy

STORY LINE: Lois provided instruction to Timothy when he was a child

READ IT IN THE BIBLE: 2 Timothy 1:3–7; 3:10–16

of Timothy. Likely she came to Christ during Paul's first missionary journey to Lystra, where she lived with her family. Beyond that, we know very little about her, except this: Lois' daughter married a Greek, not a Jew. He was not a believer in Jesus the Messiah. He could not perform the task of a father, teaching his children about God and the Law, or about virtue and why it is important. He didn't know God; he didn't care about the Law; and he had no system of belief that imbibed virtue.

Not to worry. Enter Gramma Lois. Along with Eunice, she took it upon herself to raise Timothy in the "nurture and admonition of the Lord." She taught Timothy the Law while he was still a boy. Even Paul commented that from childhood Timothy knew the Holy Scriptures. That was Gramma's doing.

So, grandmother, don't think life has passed you by. If you are looking for an opportunity to extend your influence far beyond your years, nurture your grandchildren. When you sit with them in your rocking chair, sing songs of Jesus to them. When they want a story, tell them one of those fantastic God stories from the Bible. You, grandma, are the most influential person in raising children. Don't let computer games or television steal your privilege. Be someone special. Be a godly grandmother and use your influence to shape godly lives.

LUKE

Humble Compassion

Samaritan's Purse. World Vision. Food for the Hungry.
The list of Christian humanitarian organizations grows
with growing population and growing need. Many of
these ministries have outstanding medical units who
treat the sick in distant lands. Do you know where

NAME: "From Lucania" or "Luminous"

DATE: 1st Century AD

IDENTIFICATION: Physician, companion of Paul, author of Luke
and Acts

STORY LINE: Luke served Paul on his 2nd and 3rd missionary
journeys

READ IT IN THE BIBLE: Acts 16:6–18; 20:1–24; 2 Timothy 4:9–13

these medical teams draw their inspiration? From a
compassionate doctor named Luke.

Early tradition records that Luke came from
Antioch in Syria, but he also has been associated with
the world–renowned teaching hospital in Ephesus.
He was a Gentile, the only non–Jewish author of a New
Testament book. He composed more than one–fourth

of the New Testament. Luke was not an eyewitness to Jesus' life, but due to his medical training he was an exacting researcher who interviewed eyewitnesses. He proved himself to be an amazingly accurate historian, as both archaeology and subsequent history confirm.

Luke, however, didn't allow his education or his achievements to go to his head. His gospel reveals that he was a humble man, deeply concerned about people. He knew that humble compassion for the sick, the lonely, and the forgotten are the true measures of a man or woman, not their parchments hanging on the wall. Little wonder Paul calls him the "beloved physician" (Colossians 4:14).

If you want to be appreciated, don't read people your resume or show them your awards. Instead, show them your compassion. Find someone who needs you today and do what Luke did—drop all pretense and just help them. Visit a shut-in. Read to a child. Drive an elderly person to a doctor's appointment. You may not be a physician, but to the person you help you will surely be beloved.

LYDIA

Hospitality

There's not much left of ancient Thyatira today, just some ruins in the center of modern Ak–Hissar, Turkey. But once this city was famous for its "purple," not the color, but a cloth beautifully dyed purple. Residents of Thyatira settled throughout the Greco–Roman world

NAME: "Of Lydia" or "Standing Pool"
DATE: 1st Century AD
IDENTIFICATION: Business woman from Thyatira who became a Christian
STORY LINE: Upon trusting Christ she provided lodging for the apostles
READ IT IN THE BIBLE: Acts 16:6–15

and became distributors of their hometown cloth. One of them was a woman named Lydia.

When Paul and his entourage reached Philippi, Lydia was already a "God–fearer." That means while not Jewish, she nonetheless worshiped the God of the Jews. When Paul preached the gospel in her town, God opened her heart, and Lydia believed in Jesus as

Messiah and Savior. She became the first convert to Christianity in Europe.

Maintaining your Christian testimony in business is not easy. It never has been. But as a Christian businesswoman, Lydia chose success as a Christian over success in the business world, and God gave her both. Upon embracing the gospel, Lydia did two things that could have adversely affected her bottom line. First, she chose to identify with Jesus Christ through baptism. And second, she immediately inconvenienced herself by opening her home to Paul and his fellow travelers.

That Lydia had a home large enough to accommodate multiple guests proves she did well in business. That she would use what God gave her to further the work of the gospel proves she did well in the Lord.

If God has blessed you in business, take a page from Lydia's story. Find special ways to be a blessing to those who minister the Word to you and others. Who knows? Hospitality and support may become your most important business.

MALACHI

Robbing God

There are many ways to be robbed today. Pesky telemarketers rob you of privacy and time. Pushy salespeople often rob you of common sense. Identity thieves steal your good name. Credit card thieves rob your good credit record.

NAME: "My Messenger"
DATE: 5th Century BC
IDENTIFICATION: Prophet and author of the last book of the Old Testament
STORY LINE: Malachi warned against robbing God of tithes and offerings
READ IT IN THE BIBLE: Malachi 3:6–18

You may be painfully aware that you can be robbed, but did you know God can be robbed, too? In fact, God often is robbed by the people who owe Him the most. Sometimes we rob Him of the glory that is due His name. We rob Him of our friendship, our service, our intimacy. Most often, though, we rob Him through simple neglect.

Malachi was an Old Testament prophet and author of the Bible book that bears his name. Apparently he prophesied after the Captivity. We know little or nothing about him, except that he was greatly concerned about people robbing God. He recorded God's challenge to Israel: "Will a man rob God? Yet you have robbed Me! But you say, 'In what way have we robbed You?' In tithes and offerings" (Malachi 3:8).

Is it possible you're robbing God? Are you careful to give to Him and His work cheerfully, abundantly, systematically, spontaneously, willingly? Most Christians would say yes, but recent research shows that only about two percent of evangelical believers actually tithe their income to God. Are you one of those two percent? Or are you one of the majority who say they do, but do nothing? Abundant blessings come with obedience, but when we rob God of our tithes and offerings, how can we expect Him to bless us? Think about it. Are you a giver or a grabber?

MANASSEH

Making a Comeback

In 1978, Velma Barfield murdered four people, including her mother and fiancé. But before she became the first woman executed in the U.S. in twenty–two years, Velma heard the gospel on a Christian radio station and was gloriously saved.

NAME: "Causing to Forget"
DATE: 7th Century BC
IDENTIFICATION: 13th king of Southern Kingdom; son of Hezekiah
STORY LINE: Judah's most wicked king discovers the joy of repentance
READ IT IN THE BIBLE: 2 Chronicles 33:1–20

She was genuinely repentant for her sin, and everybody in the prison knew it.

Repentance is a rare component in many stories of failure today. People sin, make a quick apology, and expect to return to their former life without consequence. But Velma knew better.

Manasseh was without question the most wicked

king Judah ever had. He murdered to maintain his control. He rebuilt the high places of pagan worship that his father had removed. Manasseh encouraged the worship of Baal and even burned one of his sons as a child sacrifice. He was ruthless, incorrigible, seemingly irredeemable, and a perfect candidate for God's grace.

When Manasseh was taken to Babylon as a prisoner of war, he came to grips with his sin and genuinely repented. So changed was he that Manasseh wanted to make things right, and God gave him the chance. He was restored as king and abolished all the pagan practices he had set in place.

Manasseh was the longest reigning king in either Judah or Israel. Unfortunately, he was the most notorious king as well. But when God changes a life, He changes it for the better. What He did for Manasseh, He can do for someone you know. Pray that they will come to grips with their sin, be broken by it, and ask God to restore them. They can begin a brand new life, forgiven and restored. If Manasseh can, anybody can.

MARK

Getting a Second Chance

The shadows around John Mark were long because the people around him were tall. His mother, Mary, was a wealthy woman of Jerusalem in whose house the church prayed. Cousin Barnabas was an apostle and trusted envoy of Jerusalem's church. And then there

NAME: "Polite" or "Shining"

DATE: 1st Century AD

IDENTIFICATION: Cousin of Barnabas, Mark was an associate of Peter and Paul

STORY LINE: Mark abandoned Paul on his first missionary journey

READ IT IN THE BIBLE: Acts 13:1–13

was Peter—Mark trusted Christ under Peter's influence. And finally, Paul. What a long shadow he cast over Mark's life.

Mark was young and ready to take on any challenge. Paul, Barnabas, and he set sail for Cyprus and then on to Asia Minor. There something went terribly wrong. When they docked at Perga, Mark gave up the journey. We don't know why, but he went home. This caused such a rift between Paul and Barnabas that on the second missionary journey Paul refused to take Mark along (Acts 15:36–41.

So, was that it? Did Mark's ministry career crash and burn on the first try? We don't hear about him for another ten years, then suddenly Paul asked the Colossians to welcome Mark as a fellow laborer. During his Roman imprisonment, virtually all alone, the apostle who cast the long shadow wrote to Timothy and said, "Get Mark and bring him with you, for he is useful to me for ministry" (2 Timothy 4:11).

Sometimes we think when we make foolish mistakes early in life that our usability to the Lord is over. But that's never true. Ask John Mark. Yes, he blew his first assignment, but the God of grace gave him new assignments and those he passed with flying colors. If you've blown an assignment for God, ask Him to forgive you and give you another chance. He will. He's just that kind of God.

MARTHA

Intimacy Precedes Activity

The hardest thing about personal devotions is finding the time to have them. So many things need to be done that somehow a quiet time with God gets shoved aside.

Mary, Martha, and Lazarus lived in Bethany. They

NAME: "Lady" or "Mistress"
DATE: 1st Century AD
IDENTIFICATION: Sister of Mary and Lazarus; resident of Bethany
STORY LINE: Martha allowed service to replace her worship of Jesus
READ IT IN THE BIBLE: Luke 10:38–42

were close friends of the Lord Jesus. Once when Jesus was visiting their house, while everyone clung to each word He taught, Martha was busy preparing and serving the meal. Others didn't seem to care that when Jesus finished teaching, they all would want to eat. *Food doesn't just magically appear on the table,* Martha must have thought.

When she had all she could take, Martha complained to Jesus about the lack of help. Martha expected Jesus to be sympathetic and He was, but in His response He gave us a life principle that many busy servants of the Lord forget. "Martha, Martha, you are worried and troubled about many things. But one thing is needed, and Mary has chosen that good part, which will not be taken away from her" (Luke 10:41,42).

Martha understood the principle of service, but missed the principle of intimacy. She had her hands full preparing and serving, but Mary had her heart full loving and learning. Jesus knew that everything Martha did was necessary and was done for Him, but He challenged her to reorder her priorities.

We dare not allow our outward activities for the Lord to hinder our inward adoration of Him. Because of Martha's focus on the work, she was failing to take pleasure in the worship the others enjoyed. Intimacy must always precede activity. Spend quality time with the Lord daily and let your recharged batteries energize your service to Him.

MARY

Honor or Worship

The Bible doesn't tell us much about Mary. She was a young virgin of the tribe of Judah and in the line of David. She was engaged to a carpenter named Joseph. Life was hard but quite normal. Then everything changed.

NAME: "Sea of Bitterness"
DATE: 1st Century AD
IDENTIFICATION: Virgin girl of Nazareth; wife of Joseph, mother of Jesus
STORY LINE: Mary was honored by God to bear the long-awaited Messiah
READ IT IN THE BIBLE: Luke 1:26–38

The angel Gabriel came to Mary and informed her that she would bear a child, but not by Joseph. This child would be the Son of the Highest, the Messiah of Israel, the Savior of all mankind. Gabriel said to Mary, "Rejoice, highly favored one, the Lord is with you; blessed are you among women" (Luke 1:28).

It is obvious that Mary was virtuous. But the favor that God brought to her—to bear the Christ child—was a gift of God's grace, not a reward for her virtue. The expression "highly favored" in the Greek language is the perfect passive participle. It means that Mary was made agreeable to God to bear the baby Jesus. It's the same expression used in Ephesians 1:6 describing believers as being made "accepted" in the Beloved. It is all of God's grace, not our goodness.

Was Mary a special young lady? She certainly was. Was she sinless like the Savior? She certainly wasn't. But God honored her to be the mother of the One who would take away the sins of the world, and for that reason we honor her as well. But honor and worship are different. We honor Mary; we worship Jesus. Honor belongs to those God chooses to use; worship belongs only to God. Make sure your worship is directed toward God today. That's where Mary's worship is targeted.

MARY MAGDALENE

Quiet Devotion

Devotion. Dedication. Dependability. Disciple. Words that describe Mary Magdalene. Mary had her problems, but being a prostitute wasn't one of them. Some have mistakenly thought she was the woman Jesus rescued from stoning in Luke 7 because her

NAME: "Sea of Bitterness"
DATE: 1st Century AD
IDENTIFICATION: Woman from Magdala out of whom Jesus cast 7 demons
STORY LINE: Mary Magdalene's devotion was rewarded at the tomb
READ IT IN THE BIBLE: John 20:1–18

story follows in the next chapter. The woman caught in adultery wasn't Mary, but she was harassed by seven demonic spirits until Jesus healed her (Luke 8:2). After that she joined the band of disciples and followed Jesus wherever He went. She was there when Jesus was tried. She was there as He carried His cross on the Via Dolorosa. She was there at Calvary.

When the men fled, Mary stayed by the foot of the cross ready to minister to her Savior.

God has a very good memory; He rewards this kind of faithfulness. Mary Magdalene was not a preacher, an apostle, or a leader of the church. She was a simple woman who was wholly devoted to her Savior, and God didn't forget that. When the women came to the empty tomb, they ran to tell Peter and John who returned to see for themselves. Then all but Mary left. She lingered. In the quietness of that moment, Jesus stepped from the shadows and called her by name (John 20:16). Mary's name—the first recorded words of the resurrected Lord. Mary Magdalene—the first person to see the risen Savior. God rewards our devotion to Him.

You don't have to be a headliner to be devoted to Jesus. But quiet devotion often pays dividends headliners never know. If you want to enjoy God's dividends today, give Him your complete devotion. It's a good investment because God doesn't forget.

MARY

Dreaming or Doing

In the book *Men Are From Mars, Women Are From Venus*, author John Gray explores how men and women are very different. The Bible bears that out, especially in how men and women expressed their love for the Lord Jesus.

NAME: "Sea of Bitterness"
DATE: 1st Century AD
IDENTIFICATION: Sister of Martha and Lazarus; resident of Bethany
STORY LINE: Mary's devotion to Jesus is a pattern for all who follow her
READ IT IN THE BIBLE: Mark 14:1–9; John 12:1–8

Jesus and His disciples were in Bethany just before He was crucified. In a lovely expression of her devotion, Mary took an alabaster flask of very costly spikenard and poured the expensive perfume over Jesus' head. She gave her Savior the best she had. And not just a dab here or there, she gave Him all she had. Immediately her selfless act was criticized by some of the male disciples as a waste. But it was no waste to Jesus. He defended Mary saying, "She has done what she could" (Mark 14:8).

Often men and women express their devotion to the Savior in different ways. That's the way it should be. Mary knew she wasn't Peter or James; she was Mary, but she did what she could and that pleased the Lord so much He promised, "Wherever this gospel is preached in the whole world, what this woman has done will also be told as a memorial to her" (Mark 14:9).

Are you dreaming of doing big things for God? Are you loaded with potential and just waiting for your big break? Forget it. That break may never come. What's already here, however, is an opportunity for you to do what you can. That's all the Savior asks of both men and women. If you do what you can, you'll have accomplished much more than those who only dream of doing big things for God. Remember, doing is always better than dreaming.

MATTHEW

Changing Jobs

Do you know what are the most desirable occupations today? According to a recent poll, number one is Web site manager. The top ten included computer systems analyst, software engineer, computer programmer,

---

NAME: "Gift of Jehovah"
DATE: 1st Century AD
IDENTIFICATION: Son of Alphaeus, tax collector; also called Levi
STORY LINE: Called to discipleship while working his Galilee tax booth
READ IT IN THE BIBLE: Matthew 9:9–13; Mark 2:13–17

---

and Web developer. Protestant minister came in at number fifty–one.

One of the most hated occupations in Jesus' day was tax collector. Matthew should know; that's what he was before he became one of Jesus' twelve apostles. Jesus ranked tax collectors with murderers and robbers and lumped them with harlots (Matthew 21:31), heathens (18:17), and other sinners (9:10).

Tax collectors were hated, viewed as scabs on society, because they were contracted by the Roman government to collect local and transportation taxes. They would agree to pay a pre–arranged sum for the right to collect taxes. Matthew collected taxes around Capernaum in Galilee. He made his money by squeezing from the public every last penny he could and keeping whatever was more than he agreed to pay the government.

How dreary Matthew's life must have been, but one day Jesus changed all that. He called Matthew to leave collecting taxes for Herod Antipas and follow Him. Matthew obeyed the Master's call, and his life would never be the same.

Are you unhappy with your job? Maybe it's because God doesn't want you there. Just wanting to improve your life doesn't mean you are called to full-time service for the Lord, but if you think God may have more for you, talk with your pastor. Pray and ask God to reveal His will to you. Who knows? You may be spinning your wheels now, but you could be changing the world in the future.

MEPHIBOSHETH

Covered by Fine Linen

Mephibosheth was only five years old when his father, Jonathan, and his grandfather, Saul, died on Mount Gilboa in the Battle of Jezreel. When the news reached the Israelite palace, Mephibosheth's nurse scooped up the infant and ran for safety. In the

NAME: "Reproach from My Mouth"
DATE: 10th Century BC
IDENTIFICATION: Son of Jonathan and grandson of Saul; also called Merib–Baal
STORY LINE: David showed grace and kindness to Mephibosheth
READ IT IN THE BIBLE: 2 Samuel 4:4; 9:1–13

process, the boy was dropped accidentally and became lame for life.

After David became king, he wanted to show kindness to the descendants of Saul. That's when he learned that his friend Jonathan had a son living in the house of Machir in Lo Debar. David summoned Mephibosheth to his palace, welcomed him to his home, appointed servants for him, and gave him a seat at the royal table. The fine linen of David's table covered Mephibosheth's lame feet so no one would know of his malady.

While this act of mercy and grace is heartwarming, it is also instructive. What David did for Mephibosheth, God did for you and me. We were part of the enemy's family, but God, in His grace, decided to show favor to us. He sought us, discovered that we were living in Lo Debar (which means "no pasture"), and brought us to His palace, treating us royally. We are still lame because of our sin, but the fine linen of God's table covers our feet the way the blood of Christ covers our sins.

Take some time today to thank God for showing His kindness to you. Without Him, like Mephibosheth, you would still be living in the desert. With Him you have the promise of righteousness and a home in heaven. And it's all because of God's amazing grace. Now that's something to praise God for.

MESHELEMIAH

Making the Menial Meaningful

Have you ever heard anyone say, "I would rather be a doorkeeper in the house of my God than dwell in the tents of wickedness"? Probably you have. That's a quote from Psalm 84:10. But have you ever met a

NAME: "Jehovah Has Recompensed"

DATE: 10th Century BC

IDENTIFICATION: A Korahite chosen to guard the east gate of the Tabernacle

STORY LINE: Gave meaning to "I would rather be a doorkeeper . . ."

READ IT IN THE BIBLE: 1 Chronicles 26:1–3, 9–19; Psalm 84

doorkeeper in the house of God? Probably you haven't. Well, meet Meshelemiah.

When King David captured Jerusalem, he made it Israel's capital city, the political center of his kingdom. But with the return of the Ark of the Covenant, one of the most important treasures of Israel, David wanted to build a temple for the ark. God, however, nixed that idea. David had been a man of war and the temple must be built by a man of peace. So David's son Solomon was given the honor of building a temple for Jehovah.

Still, David knew he could help his son get a jump on building the temple if he gathered most of the finances and materials necessary for its construction. David also drew up the blueprints. He commissioned thousands of people to be ready to build the temple and then staff it after its construction. Among those commissioned were Meshelemiah (also called Shelemiah) and his sons. They weren't priests. They weren't even Levites. They were doorkeepers (actually gatekeepers) for the temple. Anyone who wanted to enter had to be admitted by Meshelemiah's family.

Being a doorkeeper in God's house has become synonymous with doing the less spectacular work for God. If your ministry isn't flashy, remember Meshelemiah. Without him, no one would ever have gotten into the temple. What you do is important to God. Let it be important to you, too.

MICAH

Hopes and Fears

When Phillips Brooks stood in his pulpit at the Holy Trinity Church in Philadelphia, Pennsylvania, people took notice. He stood six-foot-four and was an imposing figure. Brooks visited the Holy Land in 1865

NAME: "Who is Like Jehovah?"

DATE: 8th Century BC

IDENTIFICATION: A native of Moresheth; a prophet contemporary with Isaiah

STORY LINE: He warned Judah of false hope about divine judgment

READ IT IN THE BIBLE: Micah 1:1–9; 3:9–12; 5:1–5; 7:8–20

and was particularly impressed with the Christmas Eve service at Bethlehem's Church of the Nativity.

The prophet Micah was impressed with Bethlehem, too. He pinpointed it as the place where the Messiah and Savior would be born. "But you, Bethlehem Ephrathah, though you are little among the thousands of Judah, yet out of you shall come forth to Me the One to be Ruler in Israel, whose goings forth are from of old, from everlasting" (Micah 5:2). Approximately seven hundred years before it happened, God told us exactly where Jesus would be born.

Three years after visiting the Holy Land, Phillips Brooks needed a Christmas song for his children's service, but none seemed appropriate. So, inspired by his visit to Bethlehem, he wrote one himself. "O little town of Bethlehem, how still we see thee lie; above thy deep and dreamless sleep the silent stars go by. Yet in thy dark streets shineth the everlasting Light; the hopes and fears of all the years are met in thee tonight."

Think of it. One night long ago in the little town of Bethlehem "the hopes and fears of all the years" came together in the only Person who could take away our fears and give us hope—Jesus. You don't have to wait until Christmas to thank God for what He did that night in Bethlehem. The Son of God became a man so men could become the sons of God.

MICAIAH

Telling the Truth

Remember "Baghdad Bob"? He was the amiable spokesman for Saddam Hussein during the war with Iraq. His news conferences were always upbeat and filled with reports of Iraqi successes, even when there were none. When the coalition troops encircled

NAME: "Who is Like Jehovah?"
DATE: 9th Century BC
IDENTIFICATION: Little–known prophet who predicted the death of Ahab
STORY LINE: King Ahab hated this prophet because he spoke the truth
READ IT IN THE BIBLE: 1 Kings 22:1–38

Baghdad, Bob affirmed, "There are no troops anywhere near Baghdad." Bob's reports became a joke because they never reflected reality.

Israel's King Ahab had four hundred "Yes–Men" who always told him what he wanted to hear. But there was a prophet named Micaiah who never did. Once Ahab asked King Jehoshaphat of Judah to join forces with him against the Syrians at Ramoth Gilead. Jehoshaphat wanted to make sure God would give them victory and said to Ahab, "Please inquire for the word of the LORD today" (1 Kings 22:5). Ahab's four hundred "Baghdad Bobs" all sang a chorus of victory, but Jehoshaphat wasn't impressed. He asked, "Is there not still a prophet of the Lord here, that we may inquire of Him?" (1 Kings 22:7).

There was, but Ahab admitted, "I hate him, because he does not prophesy good concerning me, but evil" (1 Kings 22:8). Micaiah always told Ahab the truth, so the king cast him into prison, but to no avail. The wicked ruler died in battle, just as Micaiah predicted.

It's not always popular to tell people the truth, especially when others are telling them what they want to hear. But would you want your doctor to paint a rosy picture of your health when you had cancer and needed immediate treatment? When faced with the choice of appeasing someone and thus endangering them or being honest and saving them, choose honesty. The end results are always more positive.

MIRIAM

The Trouble with Jealousy

The phrase "green–eyed monster" is certainly an apt description of jealousy. Few things ruin our lives faster than jealousy and bitterness. Ask Miriam.

She was the sister of Moses and Aaron. Given the task of watching her baby brother in the bulrushes,

NAME: "Bitterness" or "Rebellion"
DATE: 15th Century BC
IDENTIFICATION: Daughter of Amram and Jochebed, sister of Aaron and Moses
STORY LINE: Miriam claimed equality with Moses, became leprous
READ IT IN THE BIBLE: Numbers 12:1–16

Miriam displayed both courage and cunning. She suggested that the Egyptian princess find a Hebrew nurse for the baby, and then Miriam shrewdly found her own mother. Pharaoh paid Jochebed to care for her own baby. Called "Miriam the prophetess" in Exodus 15:20, she was one of the leaders sent by God to guide Israel (Micah 6:4).

But Miriam had a problem; Aaron, too. While they had been called to leadership, their brother Moses was doing all the main leading. When Moses married an Ethiopian wife, his siblings used this as an excuse to vent their jealousy. But the Ethiopian wife thing was a cover–up. It's mentioned in Numbers 12:1 but dropped immediately. Verse two gives Miriam's real reason for lashing out at her brother—jealousy.

Jehovah quickly moved to punish Miriam's rebellion. She became leprous, as white as snow. Shut out of the camp for seven days, Israel was stopped dead in its tracks. Nobody moved. Everyone knew the delay was because of Miriam's jealously. Moses interceded for his sister and God mercifully healed her. But sin has consequences. We do not hear of Miriam again until her death and burial at Kadesh (Numbers 20:1).

If you're feeling a bit jealous over a friend or family member, remember Miriam. Her jealousy and bitterness hurt her far more than they hurt Moses. The person jealousy hurts the most is always the jealous person.

MOSES

Time Out

Moses started out in hot water—well, warm water at least. Because the Hebrew slaves were growing in number, Pharaoh ordered that all the Hebrew boy babies be killed at birth. But Moses' mother hid him in a little basket among the reeds of the warm waters

Name: "Drawn Out"
Date: 15th Century BC
Identification: Son of Amram and Jochebed, great grandson of Levi
Story Line: Moses was chosen by God to lead Israel from bondage
Read it in the Bible: Exodus 2:1–3:17

of the Nile. When Pharaoh's daughter discovered the baby, she took him home, and Moses was raised in the palace of the most powerful man on earth.

Moses never lost his heart for his people. When he saw an Egyptian beating a Hebrew slave, he killed the Egyptian and buried him in the sand. When discovered, Moses had to flee to Midian where he spent forty years tending sheep on the backside of the desert. Here God appeared to him in a burning bush and called him to lead his people from Egyptian bondage.

Moses was such a God–enthused leader that from this rag–tag group of oppressed slaves, he built a unified nation. From the covenant given on Mount Sinai, Moses was able to found the religious community of Israel. And from his interpretation and application of God's laws, he successfully founded the religion of the Jews.

Moses spent his first forty years in the Egyptian Pharaoh's palace thinking he was somebody. Then he spent his next forty years on the backside of the Midian desert discovering he was nobody. Finally, he spent forty years leading the nation of Israel, finding out what God can do with a nobody.

If you seem to be "stuck" in your spiritual growth, don't regret your time on the backside of the desert. That's where God prepares His giants.

NEBUCHADNEZZAR

Humbling the Proud

Who can forget those graphic pictures of Saddam Hussein being fished out of his "spider hole." This once ruthless dictator suffered from delusions of grandeur. He saw himself as a second Nebuchadnezzar.

NAME: "O God Nabu, Protect My Son"
DATE: 6th Century BC
IDENTIFICATION: King of Babylonia who captured Jerusalem in 587 BC
STORY LINE: Jehovah taught this world leader a lesson in humility
READ IT IN THE BIBLE: 2 Chronicles 36:11–21; Daniel 4:1–37

Too bad Saddam didn't read what the Bible had to say about what happened to the original Nebuchadnezzar.

It's true. Nebuchadnezzar was the great and mighty king of the Babylonian Empire, ruling from 605 to 562 BC. And it's true that he humbled God's people, the Jews, when he captured Jerusalem and destroyed the Temple, carrying the people of Judah into captivity in Babylon. Nebuchadnezzar built the famous "hanging gardens" of Babylon, one of the seven wonders of the ancient world. All that Saddam Hussein believed about Nebuchadnezzar was true. But Saddam didn't read the end of the story.

When Nebuchadnezzar boasted about his accomplishments (Daniel 4:30), God humbled him at the height of his power. Nebuchadnezzar was driven from his throne and lived with the wild beasts, eating grass like an ox. His hair grew like the feathers of an eagle and his fingernails like the claws of a bird. He must have looked a lot like Saddam coming out of that "spider hole." The parallels between the ancient Nebuchadnezzar and the modern one are uncanny.

The Bible says, "Pride goes before destruction, and a haughty spirit before a fall" (Proverbs 16:18). If you notice pride growing in your personal life, take a lesson from Nebuchadnezzar, or Saddam. "God resists the proud, but gives grace to the humble" (James 4:6). It's much better to humble ourselves before God and let Him lift us up than to lift ourselves up before God and have Him humble us.

Pride goes before
destruction,
and a haughty
spirit before a fall.

—Proverbs 16:18

NEHEMIAH

Successfully Facing Opposition

You try to spend some quiet time with God, but the guy next door plays his music so loud you can't concentrate. You express your belief in a Creator, but everybody in your science class laughs at you. You attempt to witness to a co–worker, but she doesn't

NAME: "Comfort of Jehovah"

DATE: 5th Century BC

IDENTIFICATION: Artaxerxes' cupbearer who was appointed governor of Judah

STORY LINE: Nehemiah overcame all forms of opposition to be successful

READ IT IN THE BIBLE: Nehemiah 1:1–2:10

want to hear any of that religious stuff. Do you feel like you're always facing opposition? You're not alone.

Nehemiah faced multiple forms of opposition, too. He was a descendant of the Jews carried off to Babylon in 587 BC. In 539 BC Cyrus the Persian permitted the exiles to return to Jerusalem, but nearly a century later Nehemiah was still living in Persia. In

445 BC he received permission from King Artaxerxes to rebuild Jerusalem's walls.

Hardly had Nehemiah arrived in Jerusalem when Sanballat the Horonite, Tobiah the Ammonite, and Geshem the Arab began harassing him. Their tactics included ridicule (Nehemiah 2:19), conspiracy (4:9), discouragement (4:10), death threats (4:11), opportunism (5:4) diversion (6:2), slander (6:6), and more. But God sustained Nehemiah, and the wall was finished in fifty–two days.

Why was Nehemiah so successful in overcoming opposition? First, the people had a mind to work— it's hard to defeat *determined* people. Second, Nehemiah prayed that God would strengthen him for the task— it's hard to defeat *strengthened* people. And finally, everyone recognized that God was working through them—it's hard to defeat *encouraged* people.

You can successfully face your opposition if you do what Nehemiah did—be determined, ask God to strengthen you, and to work through you. God will do it. He will always be there for you. That's what He promised.

NICODEMUS

Risking Everything for Jesus

There are an estimated 300 million Dalits in India, trapped by generational poverty in Hindu's lowest caste. When a Dalit is drawn to Christ, that's cause for rejoicing—by worldly standards, the Dalit has nothing to lose and everything to gain in trusting Christ—

NAME: "Victory of the People"

DATE: 1st Century AD

IDENTIFICATION: A Pharisee and member of the Sanhedrin who followed Jesus

STORY LINE: Nicodemus' questions evoked Jesus' gospel presentation

READ IT IN THE BIBLE: John 3:1–18

but many other people around the world accept Christ at the risk of poverty, family repudiation, or job loss. For them, becoming a Christian is far more hazardous.

Nicodemus knew the risks. He was a Pharisee, a wealthy, educated, and powerful member of the Sanhedrin. By expressing faith in Christ, he had much to lose. Perhaps that's why his first encounter with Jesus was at night. Jesus informed Nicodemus that his religion was insufficient to save him; Nicodemus must be born again, born from above.

The next time Nicodemus appears in John's Gospel is when the Sanhedrin was denouncing Jesus as a false prophet. He cautioned his colleagues, "Does our law judge a man before it hears him and knows what he is doing?" (John 7:51). Nicodemus' final appearance is at the burial of Jesus when he purchased about a hundred pounds of spices to anoint Jesus' body (John 19:39). He could no longer hide his faith in Christ. Nicodemus risked everything to follow the Savior. Christian tradition holds that Nicodemus suffered persecution from hostile Jews and lost his Sanhedrin membership.

What do you have to lose by following Jesus as Savior? Whatever you give up cannot compare with what you gain, whether an "outcast" or a respected community leader. See your salvation as nothing but unbelievable gain, and you'll never fail to enjoy it.

NOAH

The Ark of Salvation

Everybody knows the story of Noah and his ark. Noah's ark has become one of today's major collectables. But there's much more to the ark than that.

Noah lived in a time much like our own. Violence and corruption were rampant. Sexual perversion was

NAME: "Rest" or "Relief"
DATE: Unknown; early BC
IDENTIFICATION: Son of Lamech, built ark to save his family from the Flood
STORY LINE: Noah's ark was a perfect picture of God's salvation
READ IT IN THE BIBLE: Genesis 6:9–7:23

everywhere. "The LORD saw that the wickedness of man was great in the earth, and that every intent of the thoughts of his heart was only evil continually" (Genesis 6:5). God's holiness demanded He take action. He would destroy mankind in a universal flood.

However, there was one righteous man who walked with God. Noah found grace in the eyes of the

Lord. His family and he would be spared from destruction by an ark of God's design. Noah took two of each kind of animal into the ark to repopulate the earth when the flood waters receded.

But Noah's ark was much more than a boat. It was a picture of God's salvation. There was only one door; Jesus said "I am *the* Door" (John 10:9). God invited Noah to enter the ark; Jesus said, "If anyone enters by Me, he will be saved" (v. 9). Once Noah and his family were on board, God shut the door, enclosing them in divine safety. Jesus said, "I give them eternal life, and they shall never perish; neither shall anyone snatch them out of My hand" (v. 28).

Today we face the same choice Noah did—enter God's ark of salvation and be saved or refuse and be destroyed. Jesus is the only Savior this world will ever have. If you have entered into Him by faith, rejoice. You have a rainbow future.

ONESIMUS

Real Freedom

If you ever needed proof that there is power in the gospel, look no further than a slave named Onesimus. He served his master Philemon in the small town of Colosse. Although there is no evidence of mistreatment, nobody wants to be a slave, so

NAME: "Useful"
DATE: 1st Century AD
IDENTIFICATION: Slave living in the city of Colosse
STORY LINE: Onesimus ran away from Philemon and found Paul
READ IT IN THE BIBLE: Philemon; Colossians 4:7–9

Onesimus fled to Rome. In running away from Philemon, he ran into the apostle Paul. Paul shared his faith with him, and Onesimus became a Christian.

Paul was not sympathetic with slavery, but apparently Onesimus had stolen from Philemon and needed to make amends. Paul sent Onesimus back to Philemon with a letter indicating that Onesimus had become like a son to him. Paul implied that freeing Onesimus was Philemon's Christian duty, but he stopped short of commanding him to do so. Instead, he requested that once the slave had squared things with his master, Paul would like him to return to Rome, because Onesimus was useful to him.

When you become free in Christ, even if you aren't always free in society, the sky is the limit. Effective service to God does not depend on your status in life, only on your willingness to be useful. Many scholars believe this Onesimus is the bishop by the same name who is praised in a letter from Ignatius of Antioch to the second–century church at Ephesus. Although the gospel doesn't promise to change your status in life, it certainly will change your destiny, and sometimes a change in your life's situation is an added bonus.

If you haven't done so yet today, take a moment to thank God for the freedom you have in Christ. It's like no other freedom you'll experience.

ONESIPHORUS

Commitment

Commitment has fallen on hard times. Researcher George Barna wrote, "Commitment is viewed negatively because it limits our ability to feel independent . . . and to focus upon self gratification

NAME: "Who Brings Profit"
DATE: 1st Century AD
IDENTIFICATION: Christian from Ephesus who ministered to Paul in prison
STORY LINE: Onesiphorus eagerly searched for Paul and found him
READ IT IN THE BIBLE: 2 Timothy 1:8–18

rather than helping others." But commitment was not always this weak and self–centered.

Paul was in prison for the final time. The last letter he ever wrote was to young Timothy, and in it he praised the commitment of a man you and I know virtually nothing about—Onesiphorus.

Think of what Paul highlights about Onesiphorus' commitment in 2 Timothy 1:16–18. This obscure man proves that true commitment demands *consistency*. Onesiphorus "often refreshed" the apostle Paul, first in Ephesus and now in Rome. Whatever that means, Onesiphorus did it consistently.

True commitment demands *initiative*. Onesiphorus came to Rome to find Paul. "He sought me out," Paul says. Commitment always begins with the subject, not the object. If the object (your spouse, your church, your Savior) is worthy of commitment, they will be worthy whether you are committed to them or not.

True commitment demands *determination*. Paul's friend sought him out very zealously until he "found" him. Onesiphorus could easily have given up, but he wasn't going to be content to hear the Savior say, "Well tried, good and faithful servant." He wanted "Well done!"

What are you committed to today? Does your commitment exhibit the qualities of Onesiphorus? If not, reexamine the quality of your commitment and do whatever the Spirit of God tells you. Just because commitment has fallen on hard times doesn't mean it can't flourish in you.

PAUL

Completely Yielded

Henry Varley remarked, "The world has yet to see what God can do with . . . a man who is fully and wholly consecrated to Christ."

Perhaps the closest this world has seen to a wholly consecrated man, other than Jesus, was the apostle Paul.

NAME: "Small" or "Humble"
DATE: 1st Century AD
IDENTIFICATION: Benjamite from Tarsus, became an apostle of the Lord Jesus
STORY LINE: Paul tirelessly worked to take the Gospel to the Gentile world
READ IT IN THE BIBLE: Acts 9:1–22; Philippians 3:1–11

Born of Jewish parents in Tarsus, he was likely named Gaius Julius Paulus at birth. But as a strict Pharisee, his Roman citizenship was less important to him than his zeal for the Law. He would be known as Saul of Tarsus.

But one day something happened to him on the road to Damascus. The Pharisee Saul encountered the saving Christ and became the apostle Paul, a Messianic

Jew, completely devoted to Jesus of Nazareth. The Spirit of God used him to formulate a Christian theology and also to pen twenty–five percent of the New Testament.

Paul endured incredible hardships for his faith. Several times he nearly died in the Mediterranean when his ship broke apart. He was beaten, robbed, stoned, and left for dead. He gave up all that he prized to gain all that his Savior prized. Finally, he was beheaded in Rome by the Emperor Nero.

Be encouraged by the apostle's persuasion "that neither death nor life, nor angels nor principalities nor powers, nor things present nor things to come, nor height nor depth, nor any other created thing, shall be able to separate us from the love of God which is in Christ Jesus our Lord" (Romans 8:38–39).

You, too, can be more than a conqueror. Be persuaded of God's love for you, and let the world see what God can do with one person completely yielded to Him.

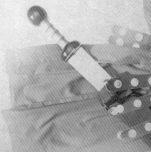

PETER
Restored

For more than four decades I have traveled to Europe on a regular basis. One of my favorite stops is the Sistine Chapel in Rome. Some years ago a complete restoration of the world's most famous ceiling was undertaken, but not without controversy. Some experts

NAME: "Stone"
DATE: 1st Century AD
IDENTIFICATION: Bethsaida fisherman; became chief disciple of Jesus
STORY LINE: Peter promised to be faithful, but denied Jesus anyway
READ IT IN THE BIBLE: Matthew 26:31–75; John 21:15–19

thought the attempted restoration would destroy the famous painting. Instead, it gave Michelangelo's masterpiece a new vibrancy.

Restoration is good for people as well as paintings. Ask Peter. Peter made his home in Bethsaida on the northern shore of the Sea of Galilee. He was the first disciple Jesus called, and his name heads every list of the

Twelve in the New Testament. Peter had a strong personality and often served as the disciples' spokesman.

But Peter was impetuous, often speaking before he thought. When Jesus predicted all His disciples would abandon Him on the night before His crucifixion, impulsive Peter objected—the others, maybe, but not him—yet within hours Peter denied his Lord three times.

While Jesus hung on the cross, Peter must have felt lower than a snake's belly. But after Jesus' resurrection the disciples went to Galilee to await a rendezvous with their Lord. There Jesus asked Peter three times if he loved Him, the same number of times Peter denied His Lord. Peter's confidence was restored by Jesus' tender words. He became the principal preacher of Christianity in the first century.

If you have done something so horrible that you think you can never be restored by the Lord, think again. Peter is the forever example of God's power to restore those who fail. He can restore you too, if you ask Him.

PHILIP

Making a Comeback

East Carolina played Marshall in the 2001 GMAC Bowl. At halftime, East Carolina had a 38–8 edge. But Marshall quarterback Bryon Leftwich orchestrated an incredible comeback, tossing an 8–yard touchdown pass in the second overtime to stun East Carolina, 64–61.

NAME: "Lover of Horses"
DATE: 1st Century AD
IDENTIFICATION: A native of Bethsaida, Philip became one of Jesus' Twelve
STORY LINE: When God wanted faith, all Philip could give Him were facts
READ IT IN THE BIBLE: John 1:43–49; 6:1–13; 14:1–12

Comebacks are always exciting, especially with people. Take Philip, for example.

Philip was one of Jesus' Twelve, a native of Bethsaida. When Philip first met Jesus he eagerly embraced the Savior. In his fledgling faith, Philip quickly found Nathanael and introduced him to the Lord, too. But at the feeding of the five thousand,

Philip's faith faltered. Jesus tested him with a question about where they could find enough bread to feed everyone. Philip answered, "Two hundred denarii worth of bread is not sufficient for them" (John 6:7). Philip's calculations were almost dead on, but while Jesus was looking for faith, all Philip could give Him were facts.

Finally, when Jesus told His disciples, "If you had known Me, you would have known My Father also" (John 14:7), Philip's faith failed completely. He responded, "Lord, show us the Father, and it is sufficient for us."

Each time we encounter Philip in John's Gospel his faith is weaker. But thank God it didn't stay that way. After ministering in Samaria and to the Ethopian eunuch, tradition tells us that he settled in Hierapolis and became "the great light of Asia (Minor)."

How's your faith today? Do you need to make a comeback? When Jesus is looking for faith, do you just give Him facts? Show Him by your life that you believe all things are possible with God.

PHOEBE

Proving Yourself Trustworthy

What do Avon, Hewlett–Packard, Xerox, eBay, and Lucent Technologies all have in common? They all have female CEOs. While women make up half the work force in the world today, they still head only a small number of businesses. Still, there have always

been businesswomen in the workplace. In the Bible, one of them was named Phoebe.

In his final chapter of Romans, Paul called Phoebe a "servant of the church in Cenchrea." Cenchrea was the eastern port of the city of Corinth, Greece. The word Paul used for "servant" was *diakonos,* meaning "deacon." Apparently Phoebe worked faithfully in daily ministration of the local church, helping many people including Paul.

When Paul wanted to send his most treasured letter to the church at Rome, he asked Phoebe to carry it for him. Three reasons. First, while the Roman Empire had a highly developed postal system, it was for official use only. Private citizens had to send their letters the old-fashioned way, by hand. Second, Phoebe's service to her church proved that she was reliable and could be trusted to deliver the Epistle to the Romans. And third, as a businesswoman, Phoebe apparently had business in Rome and was planning a trip there anyway. Paul just piggybacked on her plans. He asked the Romans to receive her and assist her in her business in Rome.

How trustworthy have you proven yourself in service to your church? Are you ready for greater responsibility? Remember, responsibility is earned one faithful task at a time. Jesus said, "Well done, good and faithful servant; you were faithful over a few things, I will make you ruler over many things" (Matthew 25:21).

PILATE

Character

New Testament scholar Brooke Foss Westcott observed: "Great occasions do not make heroes or cowards; they simply unveil them to the eyes of men. Silently and imperceptibly, as we wake or sleep, we grow strong or we grow weak, and at last some crisis

NAME: "Armed with a Dart"
DATE: 1st Century AD
IDENTIFICATION: 5th Roman procurator of Judea; ordered Jesus' crucifixion
STORY LINE: Pilate knew Jesus was innocent; ordered His death anyway
READ IT IN THE BIBLE: Matthew 27:11–26; John 18:28–19:16

shows us what we have become." Nowhere is this more evident than in the life of Pontius Pilate.

Pontius Pilate was governor of Judea and Samaria from AD 26–36. His lack of character is well attested by Tacitus, Josephus, Eusebius, and Philo. But nowhere is there a clearer picture of the kind of man Pilate was than in the Gospels.

Because the Jewish authorities could not execute a person without Rome's approval, they brought Jesus to Pilate for sentencing. Pilate questioned the Savior and concluded, "I find no fault in Him at all" (John 18:38). But the mob wanted blood so Pilate scourged Jesus, the soldiers mercilessly beat Him, and Pilate again presented Him to the mob saying, "Behold, I am bringing Him out to you, that you may know that I find no fault in Him" (19:4). When the mob yelled "Crucify Him, crucify Him!" Pilate responded again, "You take Him and crucify Him, for I find no fault in Him" (19:6). Finally, Pilate washed his hands and said, "I am innocent of the blood of this just Person" (Matthew 27:24).

Pilate knew what was right but didn't have the backbone to do it. Reputation is precious, but character is priceless. How much character will your family and friends see in you today? Ask God to give you the strength to do what you know is right. Everyone will appreciate it.

PRISCILLA

Couples

One of the great joys of ministry is when couples complement each other in the Lord. When you hear the name of one, you think of the other. Billy and Ruth Graham. Jim and Carol Cymbala. James and Shirley Dobson. The most prominent husband and

NAME: "Ancient"
DATE: 1st Century AD
IDENTIFICATION: Wife of tentmaker Aquila and supporter of Paul
STORY LINE: This husband and wife team were invaluable to Paul
READ IT IN THE BIBLE: Acts 18:1–21; Romans 16:3–5

wife team in the Bible was Priscilla and Aquila, who were friends and possibly even converts of Paul.

Aquila was a native of Pontus in Asia Minor. Priscilla, or Prisca for short, and he were expelled from Rome by an edict of the Roman Emperor Claudius in AD 49 (Acts 18:2). From Rome they settled in Corinth, where they met Paul on his second missionary journey. Working together as tentmakers enabled them to be privately tutored by the great apostle. So well–schooled were Priscilla and Aquila that they instructed the learned Apollos when he visited Corinth (Acts 18:24–28).

From Corinth they accompanied Paul to Ephesus, where they still were when he wrote First Corinthians. Their home was the meeting place for Ephesian Christians. When Claudius' edict was lifted, Priscilla and Aquila returned to Rome, where they were ministering when Paul wrote to the church there. But with Paul's last letter (2 Timothy) they were back in Ephesus.

As a tribute to their strong marriage, Priscilla and Aquila are never mentioned separately in the Bible. Priscilla's contribution was equal to her husband's, and that is evidenced by the fact that her name is mentioned before his in four out of six New Testament references.

Are you a Lone Ranger Christian when you could be a Priscilla and Aquila couple? Discover the joy of growing together as husband and wife, ministering together as a couple. Nothing will strengthen your marriage more.

QUIRINIUS

Verifying God's Word

When God's authors recorded important events in the Bible, they often took time to verify their accuracy. One way was by referring to historical events generally known apart from the Bible. Another way was by mentioning historical figures who could be dated

NAME: "One Who Governs"

DATE: 1st Century AD

IDENTIFICATION: Roman governor of Syria during the time of Jesus' birth

STORY LINE: Quirinius supervised the Roman census in his region

READ IT IN THE BIBLE: Luke 2:1–20

apart from the Bible. Some events were so important the Bible writer would double–reference or even triple–reference the event, intersecting two or three historical people to pinpoint an event. Such was the case with the birth of Jesus.

Luke records, "And it came to pass in those days that a decree went out from Caesar Augustus that all the world should be registered. This census first took place while Quirinius was governing Syria" (Luke 2:1–2). The first intersecting life at Jesus' birth was Caesar Augustus who ruled Rome from 44 BC until AD 14. But the census registration that brought Mary and Joseph to Bethlehem also occurred when Quirinius was governor of Syria. That's intersecting life number two.

According to the Roman historian Tacitus (Annals 3.48), Publius Sulpicius Quirinius was elected consul of Syria in 12 BC. Around 7 BC, he became governor of Syria during the reign of Herod the Great, the third intersecting life dating Jesus' birth. Since Quirinius became governor of Syria in 7 BC and Herod died at Jericho in the spring of 4 BC, the birth of Jesus had to be sometime from 7 BC to 4 BC.

How masterfully accurate God's Word is! The more we read it, the more reasons we have to be convinced of its veracity and accuracy. Take some time today to mine the gold that is found only in God's Word.

RAHAB

The Reach of Grace

Arthur was released from prison at age 53, having spent 42 years behind bars. He served 17 months on death row, 24 years in solitary confinement and 31 months on Devil's Island in a 5–foot by 7–foot cell, chained by his neck. But something happened to

NAME: "Spacious"

DATE: 15th Century BC

IDENTIFICATION: Prostitute and the heroine of the battle of Jericho

STORY LINE: Rahab housed two spies; was rewarded with deliverance

READ IT IN THE BIBLE: Joshua 2:1–24; 6:12–25

Arthur in Leavenworth. A preacher visited the prison with his 14–year old son, Timmy. As they passed Arthur's cell, Timmy smiled at him, and the inmate responded with a verbal tirade.

But soon Arthur began receiving letters from Timmy indicating that he loved Arthur and was praying for him. The letters continued for seven years, and finally

Arthur couldn't take it any more. He broke down and said, "I got down on my knees and trusted Christ."

Is anyone too far gone to experience the grace of God? Arthur wasn't, and neither was Rahab.

Joshua sent spies to scout out Jericho before Israel entered the Promised Land. They found their way to Rahab's inn seeking information. Rahab was a prostitute, but God was working in her heart. She hid the spies in the stalks of flax on her roof and then hung a scarlet cord from her window. That was the sign that someone lived there who had faith in Jehovah. Amazingly, this prostitute became a great–grandmother of King David, and consequently an ancestor of King Jesus (Joshua 2:1–21; 6:17–25; Matthew 1:5).

If you feel that what you've done is too heinous, too awful for God to forgive you, think again. If Rahab can find her way into Jesus' family tree, you can find your way into God's family. No one is beyond the reach of God's grace, not Rahab, not Arthur, not you.

RUTH

The Glue of Family

"A family is more than the sum of its parts," says Kay Shurden. "It is a living, shaping, powerful unit that teaches us our most important lessons in life. It teaches us who we are, how to act, whom to relate to, and what is important in life."

NAME: "Friendship"
DATE: 11th Century BC
IDENTIFICATION: Moabitess widow who married Boaz, became David's ancestor
STORY LINE: Ruth refused to break up her family, God rewarded her
READ IT IN THE BIBLE: Ruth 1:1–18; 4:9–22

Elimelech took his family—wife, Naomi, and sons, Mahlon and Chilion,—to Moab because of a severe famine in Bethlehem. There his sons married Moabite girls Ruth and Orpah. Then Elimelech and his sons died, and the three widows were traumatized. Naomi wanted to return to Bethlehem, but Orpah opted to stay in Moab. That produced one of the strangest families ever—Naomi and Ruth, a Jewish mother–in–law and a foreign daughter–in–law.

Their prospects for success were dismal, but they were a family and refused to be torn apart. When Naomi suggested Ruth remain in Moab too, Ruth replied, "Entreat me not to leave you . . . for wherever you go, I will go, and wherever you lodge, I will lodge . . ." (Ruth 1:16). There was no turning back. They would face the future together.

Families need each other. We learn from each other. We are glued with a kind of super glue that enables us to stick together to find solutions to family challenges.

If you have family members counting on you, don't see that as an obstacle; see it as an opportunity to minister to the people who need you most, and will appreciate you most—your family. God never created anything more precious than a family. As Rudyard Kipling wrote: "No person is ever alone who is a member of a family."

SAMSON

Moral Weakness

The first Olympics were not held in Greece until 776 BC, but had they been held in Samson's day, he surely would have taken gold in the weight lifting event. Samson was the world's strongest man, but his physical strength was no match for his moral

NAME: "Sun"
DATE: 11th Century BC
IDENTIFICATION: Son of Manoah, fallen hero of Israel; last of the judges
STORY LINE: Physical strength is no match for moral weakness
READ IT IN THE BIBLE: Judges 14:1–3; 16:1–20

weakness. Samson's life was marred by his insatiable desire for pagan women.

Samson insisted on marrying a young Philistine woman, in spite of his parents' objection. On another occasion he was almost captured by the Philistines while visiting a prostitute in Gaza. Eventually Samson hooked up with Delilah, and you know the rest of that story.

Samson didn't start out bad. In fact, he was set apart as a Nazirite at birth, and the Spirit of the Lord moved upon him. But in the end Samson's immoral character caught up with him. The Philistines seized him, gouged out his eyes, and bound him with bronze fetters, and took him to Gaza to grind at a mill.

Samson didn't become a moral failure because of his physical strength. It was his physical strength that revealed the failure of his moral character. If you pump a little iron to increase your strength today, don't forget about your character. What will you do today to strengthen your moral character? One day something will reveal what you have become little by little. Today's the day to begin preparing for that day.

SAPPHIRA

Honesty is the Only Policy

The hit movie *Catch Me If You Can* was based on the life of Frank Abagnale. Between the ages of 16 and 21 he bilked various organizations out of more than $2.5 million dollars by posing as an airline pilot, a medical doctor, an attorney, and a college professor.

NAME: "Beautiful" or "Sapphire"
DATE: 1st Century AD
IDENTIFICATION: Dishonest woman in the Jerusalem church; wife of Ananias
STORY LINE: This couple did not honestly represent a gift to God
READ IT IN THE BIBLE: Acts 5:1–11

Abagnale's life proves it's not always necessary to lie in order to be untruthful. All you have to do is misrepresent the truth. That's what Ananias and Sapphira did in the church at Jerusalem.

The early church financially depended on the generosity of its members. It was not required that people sell property and turn the money over to the church, but it was not uncommon either.

Sapphira and her husband, Ananias, watched others give generously, and they decided to do the same. But once they committed to give, they suffered from "giver's grief," a kind of "buyer's remorse." They began to wonder if they could afford to be so generous. They didn't have to give it all, mind you; in fact, they didn't have to give anything. Ananias and Sapphira's sin was not in giving only part of the money to the church, but in misrepresenting that they had given everything.

As a result of their deceit, both of them died and were carried out and buried immediately. The rest of the church watched in hushed astonishment.

If you have something to give to God today, be honest about it. If you have something to provide for others, don't misrepresent it. People will appreciate you much more for your honesty than for your ostentation. Be yourself. That's all God asks.

SARAH

Inner Beauty

Despite a relatively weak economy, in 2003 the cosmetics industry in the United States grew to over $45 billion dollars annually. The quest for beauty and youth doesn't come cheap.

NAME: "Princess"
DATE: 22nd Century BC
IDENTIFICATION: Wife of Abraham and mother of Isaac; originally "Sarai"
STORY LINE: Sarah proved to be an odd mix of faith and doubt
READ IT IN THE BIBLE: Genesis 18:1–15; 21:1–7; 1 Peter 3:1–6

But when I think of Sarah in the Bible, two words come to mind—"beautiful" and "old." So great was her beauty—at age 65—that Abraham feared for his life when they went to Egypt (Genesis 12:11–14). She was 75 when her impatience with God prompted her to give Hagar to Abraham as a wife. But when Sarah was 90 years old, God kept His promise and she gave birth to Isaac, the child of promise. Sarah died at age 127, the only woman in the Bible whose age was recorded at death—a sign of her great importance to the Hebrew nation.

"Old" and "beautiful." We don't often put those words together, but when the apostle Peter looked for an example of a holy woman who trusted God, possessed inward spiritual beauty, and was submissive to her husband, Sarah quickly came to mind (1 Peter 3:5–6).

It is all too easy for women to be overly concerned about their appearances, to spend too much time, energy, and money trying to make what is old look young and beautiful again. But from God's perspective, what is on the outside is not what is beautiful; it's what's on the inside. Look as good as you can, but balance that with the knowledge that God observes your heart, not just your face. Take some time today to pamper your spirit, sweeten your soul, and spruce up the beauty within you.

SAUL
Have Patience

According to one survey, if you're an average American, in your lifetime you will spend six months waiting for traffic lights to turn green, eight months opening junk mail, three years in meetings, and five years waiting in line. Little wonder our patience is wearing thin.

NAME: "Asked for" or "Demanded"
DATE: 11th Century BC
IDENTIFICATION: Benjamite; son of Kish; first king of Israel; nemesis of David
STORY LINE: Saul began well, but his impatience led to his downfall
READ IT IN THE BIBLE: 1 Samuel 15:1–22

If you struggle with a lack of patience, join the club. It's a common problem. But when impatience leads to disobedience, it's more than just a problem; it's sin. Nobody knew that better than the impatient King Saul.

Israel's first king lived during turbulent times. The twelve tribes had no unified leader, and when the Philistines threatened God's people, Saul was chosen as Israel's first king largely because of his imposing physique. He truly was a remarkable man, but his blunders overshadowed his capabilities. Most of those blunders related to his impatience.

Once, when he was about to engage the Philistines in battle as instructed by Samuel, Saul waited seven days for the prophet to arrive and make a burnt offering to God for success in the battle. But when Samuel didn't arrive when expected, Saul impatiently and unlawfully offered the sacrifice himself. As king, he was not sanctioned by God to do so, and the prophet reprimanded him saying, "You have done foolishly. . . Now your kingdom shall not continue. The LORD has sought for Himself a man after His own heart . . ." (1 Samuel 13:13–14). Saul's fate was sealed.

We all know that tribulation produces patience, but ask your Heavenly Father to give measured tribulation so you gain controlled growth in overcoming impatience. Even achieving patience takes patience.

The LORD has sought for Himself a man after His own heart.

—1 Samuel 13:13–14

SHADRACH

Never Alone

Years ago I conducted study tours for students at the university where I taught. Ordinarily I would arrange lodging ahead of time, but on one tour to England we just stopped each night at a hotel. After a while I became uneasy that no one could contact us in case of

NAME: "Command of Aku"
DATE: 6th Century BC
IDENTIFICATION: Chaldean name given to Hananiah, an early Babylonian captive
STORY LINE: Cast into fiery furnace with two friends, where four men were seen
READ IT IN THE BIBLE: Daniel 1:1–7; 3:1–30

emergency, so I called home and left a list of each town we planned to overnight in. For the first time on that tour I slept peacefully that night. My spirit was reassured, and an old song I hadn't heard in years kept coming to my mind: "Standing somewhere in the shadows you'll find Jesus."

It's good to know that God is there for you whenever you need Him. Shadrach had that experience, along with his friends Meshach and Abed-Nego. In ancient Babylon they were thrown into the fiery furnace for refusing to bow before King Nebuchadnezzar's golden image. But when the king peered into the furnace through the smoke and flames he saw something quite unexpected. He asked, "Did we not cast three men bound into the midst of the fire? . . . Look! I see four men . . . and the form of the fourth is like the Son of God" (Daniel 3:24–25).

The next time you're all alone and afraid, remember God's promise: "I will not leave you nor forsake you" (Joshua 1:5). You may not see Him, but standing somewhere in the shadows you'll find Jesus. You can always count on Him to be there when you walk through fire.

SHAMGAR

What's in Your Hand?

During World War II, American soldiers were marching through a French town when an old woman with a broom joined their ranks. The captain smiled at her and said, "You can't do much with that broom!" "No," she replied, "but I can let people know whose side I'm on."

NAME: "Stranger" or "Sword"
DATE: 13th Century BC
IDENTIFICATION: 3rd judge of Israel, son of Anath from Beth Anath in Naphtali
STORY LINE: Shamgar used an ox goad as a weapon, killing 600 Philistines
READ IT IN THE BIBLE: Judges 1:27–36; 3:31; 5:1–7

Some of God's best servants were not His best qualified or equipped. But they were His most willing. Shamgar was such a servant.

We know little or nothing about Shamgar except that God used him to stop Philistine incursions into Israel's towns. Shamgar put an end to Philistine oppression by using the only weapon he had—an ox goad.

A goad was a stick about eight feet long, tapered at one end. The slimmer end was sharpened and used for prodding the cattle. On the other end may have been a small iron wedge–shaped tip farmers used to remove the clay that stuck to the blade of their plough. An ox goad wasn't a very sophisticated weapon of war, but when wielded by a strong arm, it became a dangerous weapon. Shamgar used his ox goad to kill six hundred Philistines.

It's important that we obtain as much education as we can, gain as much skill as we can, and get as much experience as we can, but God is pleased to use anyone who will give whatever he or she has to serve Him. So what do you have? A computer? Language skills? Medical experience? A hammer? Effective service for God doesn't mean you have to possess the latest equipment, but it does mean you have to possess a willing heart. God can use whatever you give Him.

SIMEON

Seeing God's Salvation

Suppose there was a line–up of all the religious leaders in history, and you had to pick out the real deal. In the line–up were Buddha, Mohammed, Jesus, Moses, Confucius, L. Ron Hubbard, and many more. How would you tell which one was the Christ?

NAME: "Hear" or "Listen"
DATE: 1st Century AD
IDENTIFICATION: One day in the Temple Simeon worshiped the baby Jesus
STORY LINE: The Holy Spirit assured Simeon he would see the Messiah
READ IT IN THE BIBLE: Luke 2:21–35

An old man named Simeon didn't have a line–up, but he did have an opportunity to spot the Messiah of Israel. Simeon was a devout and pious man. He had waited years for his Messiah to show up in Israel but had been always been disappointed. And yet the Holy Spirit promised Simeon that he would not die until he had seen the Lord's Christ. Simeon clung to that promise.

Then one day the Spirit moved him to go to the temple. Today his long wait would be over. When Jesus' parents entered the temple with their baby in their arms, Simeon spotted Him immediately, grabbed Him up in his arms and prayed, "Lord, now You are letting Your servant depart in peace, according to Your word; for my eyes have seen Your salvation" (Luke 2:29, 30). Simeon knew there would be many religious leaders throughout history, but when he saw Jesus, he saw God's salvation.

Have you seen Jesus that way? Not as another religious leader, but as the Lord's Christ? Have you looked into the face that says to you, "I am the way, the truth, and the life. No one comes to the Father except through Me"? (John 14:6). While this world has many religions, it still has only one Savior. Simeon knew Who that was, do you? Remember God's promise: "Believe on the Lord Jesus Christ, and you will be saved" (Acts 16:31).

SIMON

Unity in Diversity

Do you recognize the names Yo–Yo Ma, Itzhak Perlman, and James Galway? They are all premier musicians.

When Yo–Yo Ma plays his cello, his music soulfully moves you. When Itzhak Perlman is handed a violin, he

Name: "Hear" or "Listen"
Date: 1st Century AD
Identification: A Cananean or Zealot who Jesus chose as a disciple
Story Line: A member of a fanatical Jewish sect is mainlined by Jesus
Read it in the Bible: Matthew 10:1–4; Mark 3:13–18; Acts 1:1–14

turns it into a gift from God. And when James Galway plays his flute, the music is smooth as silk. Individually they sound wonderful, but put them together in a symphony orchestra and their music is glorious.

Diversity that leads to harmony also leads to delight. Put together people of diverse abilities, give them a common cause, and they always produce greater strength than people with similar abilities left to themselves.

Jesus knew that. That's why among His disciples were fishermen, a tax collector, and even a zealot. Simon the Cananean was a member of a fanatical party, a political extremist, a terrorist who would do anything to end the Roman occupation of Palestine. But when he trusted Jesus Christ as Savior and followed Him as Lord, he became one of Jesus' twelve apostles.

If your background is different from others' in your Bible study group or church, don't be concerned. You have something unique to contribute just because of who you are. Just make sure that the diversity of your group doesn't become division. When there is unity in diversity there is also incredible strength.

Remember the words of the psalmist: "Behold, how good and how pleasant it is for brethren to dwell together in unity!" (Psalm 133:1). In all that you do today, let your uniqueness be a strength to bring unity. Let your life be a symphony, not a solo.

SOLOMON

Unsatisfied

What does it take to satisfy you? John D. Rockefeller was making a million dollars a week when he died, but he wasn't satisfied. King Solomon of Israel built the glorious Temple in Jerusalem. His was considered to be the "Golden Age" of Israel. Solomon's wisdom and wealth

NAME: "Peaceful"
DATE: 10th Century BC
IDENTIFICATION: Son of David; king of Israel; Temple builder; song writer
STORY LINE: Solomon was unsatisfied with wisdom, wealth, and women
READ IT IN THE BIBLE: 2 Chronicles 9:1–6; Ecclesiastes 2:1–26; 12:8

were unmatched by anyone in the ancient world, as the Queen of Sheba found out, still he was unsatisfied.

Read Solomon's own sad words: "I made my works great, I built myself houses, and planted myself vineyards . . . I acquired male and female servants . . . I had greater possessions of herds and flocks than all who were in Jerusalem before me . . . So I became great and excelled more than all . . . Then I looked on all the works that my hands had done . . . and indeed all was vanity and grasping for the wind" (Ecclesiastes 2:4,7,9,11). Solomon was horribly unsatisfied.

Enough never seems to be enough in this world. The more we have, the more we want. But there is something that God provides for you that is enough, and that's His grace. "And God is able to make all grace abound toward you, that you, always having all sufficiency in all things, may have an abundance for every good work" (2 Corinthians 9:8).

If you're restless and unsatisfied today, ponder Jesus' words: "For what will it profit a man if he gains the whole world, and loses his own soul?" (Mark 8:36). True satisfaction doesn't come from getting more things, but from accepting the grace of God and asking Him to give you eternal life.

STEPHEN

Ready to Die

John Kelly—Iraq, 2004. Martin Burnham—
Philippines, 2002. Kaleb Situmorang—Indonesia,
2000. Liu Haitong—China, 2000. Graham Staines
and his sons, Philip and Timothy—India, 1999. The

NAME: "Crown"

DATE: 1st Century AD

IDENTIFICATION: One of the first seven deacons; the first
Christian martyr

STORY LINE: A good and worthy man, Stephen paid the ultimate
sacrifice

READ IT IN THE BIBLE: Acts 6:8–7:60

list of those who have died for the cause of Christ
continues to grow.

The trail of martyrs' blood goes back to Jerusalem's
early Christian community, which consisted of two
Jewish groups divided on the basis of language and
culture. The "Hebrews" (those from Aramaic–speaking
synagogues) and the "Greeks" (those from
Greek–speaking synagogues) made up the early church.

Stephen, one of seven deacons who served those who spoke Greek, was a deeply committed man. To become a deacon you had to have a good reputation and be filled with the Holy Spirit and wisdom. But Stephen is further described as a man "full of faith and the Holy Spirit" (Acts 6:5) and also "full of faith and power" (Acts 6:8). When the Jewish leaders accused Stephen of blasphemy and dragged him before the Sanhedrin, he was summarily condemned to death. The council hustled him outside the city and threw stones at him until he was dead. Stephen became the first Christian martyr. Many more martyrs have followed ever since.

Are you willing to give your life in the cause of Christ? Don't be too quick to answer, because you might not be in a position to be asked. Remember, Stephen was a man full of wisdom, power, and the Holy Spirit. Christian martyrs aren't just in the wrong place at the wrong time. They're in God's place at God's time. Don't pity the martyrs. Live in such a way that you qualify to be one of them.

TERTIUS

Earning Friendship

Amanuensis (a–man–u–en–sis). In antiquity an amanuensis had the same job a secretary or personal assistant has today. He took dictation and wrote letters.

It was common for Roman officials to use an amanuensis. Paul appears to have dictated many of his

NAME: "Third"
DATE: 1st Century AD
IDENTIFICATION: Paul's amanuensis who wrote Paul's letter to the Romans
STORY LINE: Tertius couldn't help greeting the Romans as he wrote
READ IT IN THE BIBLE: Romans 16:17–27

letters to a personal secretary who wrote down what he said. The apostle would then check his work, make sure he said exactly what the Spirit of God impressed Paul to say, and then sign the letter or make some distinguishing mark to verify its authenticity (1 Corinthians 16:21; Colossians 4:18; 2 Thessalonians 3:17). On one occasion Paul appears to have written the entire letter himself, using large block letters, perhaps to drive home the urgency of his message to the Galatians (Galatians 6:11).

Paul used an amanuensis named Tertius in writing the letter to the Romans. In the final chapter, Paul greeted dozens of friends living in Rome. But Tertius also knew many of these people; they were his friends too. So, in the midst of writing Paul's greetings, Tertius couldn't help himself. He included a greeting of his own: "I, Tertius, who wrote this epistle, greet you in the Lord" (Romans 16:22). That done, he quickly returned to Paul's dictation.

The Bible says that, "A man who has friends must himself be friendly" (Proverbs 18:24). Friendship is not a gift; it is earned every day. It is not static. If a relationship is not constantly growing, it may be an acquaintance, but it's not friendship. Make an investment in your friendships today. Send a letter to a friend and encourage them in their faith. The investment is worth the effort.

THADDAEUS

God Knows Your Name

Do you know Alphonso D'Abruzzo or Maurice Micklewhite? Maybe not. But you do know actors Alan Alda and Michael Caine. Alphonso and Alan are the same people; so are Maurice and Michael. The actors have both a real name and a stage name.

NAME: "Heart" or "One Who Praises"
DATE: 1st Century AD
IDENTIFICATION: Jesus' disciple also called Lebbaeus and Judas the son of James
STORY LINE: Called by any of his three names, he was faithful
READ IT IN THE BIBLE: Matthew 10:1–4; Mark 3:13–19; Luke 6:12–16

Some people in the Bible had two names, too. Simon and Peter are the same person. So are Matthew and Levi.

One of Jesus' apostles had three names. Lebbaeus bore the surname (family name) Thaddaeus. Many manuscripts omit the name Lebbaeus and simply give the man's last name, but there may be good reason for including both names. When Luke listed the apostles he didn't mention either Lebbaeus or Thaddaeus but included "Judas the son of James" in his place (Luke 6:16). Acts 1:13 does the same thing. This disciple's real name must have been Judas Lebbaeus Thaddaeus, the son of James. Given that there is another Judas in the disciple's band, the last name was used to distinguish him from Judas Iscariot (John 14:22).

Was Thaddaeus worried about having multiple names? Apparently not. It may have been an inconvenience to him, but he knew God knew his name, and that's the important thing. How could God forget his name? He said, "I have inscribed you on the palms of My hands" (Isaiah 49:16). Jesus told us to "rejoice because your names are written in heaven" (Luke 10:20), and they are written "in the Book of Life" (Philippians 4:3).

If people have a difficult time remembering your name today, don't let it get you down. As long as your name is written in the Lamb's Book of Life, that's all that's important. After all, God knows your name, and He won't forget you.

THOMAS

Believing is Seeing

Most of us have experienced doubt, and that's not always bad. In his book *How to Make It to Friday*, Larry Jones writes, "There is much honest doubt that should be encouraged. Galileo doubted that the earth stood still. Copernicus doubted that the earth was the

NAME: "Twin"

DATE: 1st Century AD

IDENTIFICATION: One of Jesus' disciples called Didymus, Greek for "twin"

STORY LINE: Thomas is remembered as one who needed proof Jesus is alive

READ IT IN THE BIBLE: John 20:1–31

center of the universe. Columbus doubted that it was flat." Doubt leads to investigation, and investigation leads to discovery.

But we must never put a question mark where God has put a period. Thomas, also called Didymus (probably because he was a twin), often needed to see in order to believe. He became branded "doubting Thomas."

This disciple despaired when Jesus approached Jerusalem for the final time (John 11:16). He pressed Jesus for explanations in the upper room (John 14:5). And when the disciples claimed to have seen Jesus alive, his doubts seeped out with the words, "Unless I . . . put my finger into the print of the nails, and put my hand into His side, I will not believe" (John 20:25).

But faith is believing what you cannot see (Hebrews 11:1). Once Thomas encountered the risen Christ he exclaimed, "My Lord and my God!" (John 20:28). Jesus countered with, "Blessed are those who have not seen and yet have believed" (John 20:29). Thomas doubted no more. He appears to have taken the Gospel to India where he was martyred.

Your faith is not in the unknown; it is in the character of God with whom you can trust the unknown. If you're having trouble with your faith today, focus on God's character rather than on what you see or don't see. Faith in God is never misplaced.

TIMOTHY

Soul Mate

Cliff Barrows was on his honeymoon in 1945 when a desperate call came from a local evangelistic crusade. The song leader had become ill, and Cliff agreed to help out. The young evangelist was Billy Graham and

NAME: "Honoring God"
DATE: 1st Century AD
IDENTIFICATION: Son of Eunice, grandson of Lois, convert and associate of Paul
STORY LINE: Timothy was Paul's "soul mate," his "true son in the faith"
READ IT IN THE BIBLE: Acts 16:1–5; 1 Timothy 1:1–4; Philippians 2:19–24

the rest, as they say, is history; they've been working together ever since.

Good things are accomplished when soul mates work together. David and Jonathan were Old Testament soul mates. Paul and Timothy were New Testament ones.

Paul led Timothy to the Lord on his second missionary journey. The apostle called Timothy his "beloved and faithful son in the Lord" (1 Corinthians 4:17) and his "true son in the faith" (1 Timothy 1:2). Timothy played a prominent role in Paul's second missionary journey, and during the third missionary journey Timothy was active both in evangelizing and in correcting the problems in the Corinthian church. Also, Timothy was Paul's companion during his first imprisonment in Rome (Colossians 1:1; Philippians 1:1; Philemon 1).

But Timothy was no mere tag–along. His name is included in the salutations of 2 Corinthians, Philippians, Colossians, 1 and 2 Thessalonians, and Philemon. In writing to the Philippians, Paul hoped to send Timothy to encourage them. He said, "I have no one like–minded, who will sincerely care for your state" (Philippians 2:20). The word Paul chose means "of equal soul." They were soul mates.

Do you have someone "of equal soul" to you? If so, be grateful. That friend or spouse is a gift from God. Praise God daily for him or her. Two equal souls accomplish much more than do two partners. Partners put their minds together; soul mates put their hearts together.

TYCHICUS

An Important Team Member

I grew up watching the Pittsburgh Pirates play at Forbes Field. Like other fans of that time, I exploded in glee when Bill Mazeroski hit the home run in the bottom of the ninth of the seventh game of the 1960

NAME: "Fortuitous"

DATE: 1st Century AD

IDENTIFICATION: Christian of Asia Minor; a tireless fellow worker with Paul

STORY LINE: Tychicus traveled to Ephesus, Colosse, Crete, and more

READ IT IN THE BIBLE: Acts 20:1–6; Ephesians 6:21–24; Colossians 4:7–9

World Series to beat the Yankees. But Dick Scofield was my favorite Pirate.

Scofield was a utility infielder. Not a starter or a star, he was nevertheless invaluable to the team. He could play second base, shortstop, even third base. Utility infielders can go in for almost anybody and make a contribution.

Tychicus was the utility infielder of the early

church. A native of Ephesus, he accompanied Paul on his trip to collect the offering for the poor of the Jerusalem church (Acts 20:4). He served as the courier for Paul's letter to Ephesus (Ephesians 6:21), Colossians (Colossians 4:7), and Philemon. Probably Tychicus accompanied Trophimus and Titus to deliver Paul's second Corinthian letter (2 Corinthians 8:16–24). Later Paul sent him to Crete to assist Titus (Titus 3:12). And even later still, Paul informed Timothy that he had sent Tychicus to Ephesus (2 Timothy 4:12). Tychicus always had his bags packed, always had a job to do, and always was willing to take on any challenge.

Has God called you to be a Tychicus? Does He want you to be willing to do any job, teach any group, or be anything the church needs you to be? If so, be happy and do those things well. You may not be a starter or a star, but your contribution to the team will be enormous. Be grateful that God has a place for you on the roster.

UZZIAH

When Pride Drags You Down

British novelist Barbara Cartland began to mingle in royal circles when her daughter Raine married the 8th Earl of Spencer, father to Diana, Princess of Wales. When Cartland was interviewed by the BBC the interviewer asked if she thought that class barriers

NAME: "My Strength is Jehovah"
DATE: 8th Century BC
IDENTIFICATION: 9th king of Southern Kingdom; son of Amaziah
STORY LINE: A powerful king who failed in the end because of pride
READ IT IN THE BIBLE: 2 Chronicles 26:1–23

had finally broken down in Britain. "Of course they have," she replied, "or I wouldn't be talking to someone like you."

Proverbs 16:18 notes, "Pride goes before destruction, and a haughty spirit before a fall." It was pride that did in one of Judah's longest-reigning kings, King Uzziah.

Also called Azariah (2 Kings 14:11; 15:1–7), Uzziah was a wise and powerful ruler. His military campaigns were legendary. He broke down the walls of Gath and Ashdod and built his own cities in the heart of Philistine territory. He defeated the Arabs and forced the Ammonites to pay tribute to him. Second Chronicles 26:5 says, "as long as he sought the LORD, God made him prosper."

But in the end, Uzziah's heart became proud. He entered the Temple to burn incense. When Azariah the high priest and eighty associates confronted him, Uzziah responded in anger instead of repentance, and consequently God's judgment made him a leper.

Success often leads to pride. That's why we must always temper success with humility. If we become proud of our successes instead of using them to glorify God, those very successes can be the source of our greatest defeat. Today, thank God for every success He has given you, whether in your family, your business, your church, or your personal life. But let's not become proud of our successes. The real cause behind them is God.

VASHTI

A Challenge to Modesty

Super Bowl XXXVIII was one of the most exciting post–season NFL games ever. But the antics at the MTV–produced half time show overshadowed a great game. Many believe that exposing Janet Jackson's

NAME: "Thread"
DATE: 5th Century BC
IDENTIFICATION: Persian queen refused to exhibit herself during drunken feast
STORY LINE: Vashti proved to be a pagan with some backbone
READ IT IN THE BIBLE: Esther 1:1–22

breast on international television brought the plummeting morality of the industry to a new low.

Throughout history women have had to make difficult choices between modesty and popularity. No one displayed more courage in making that choice than did Queen Vashti. She was the beautiful queen of King Ahasuerus (Xerxes 1) who reigned over one hundred twenty–seven provinces from India to Ethiopia.

When the king sponsored a weeklong feast at his citadel palace at Shushan, he commanded his queen be brought before him wearing the royal crown. But the king and his friends were drunk and Vashti refused. The reason for her refusal is not given in the text, but the Persian historian Herodotus notes that she feared for her dignity amidst the drunken men. The Jewish Talmud also suggests that modesty was the issue. Apparently Vashti refused the king's invitation because she would not stoop to exposing herself in front of these drunken men.

Ever since Adam and Eve sinned and discovered their nakedness, God has been putting clothes on people, and Satan has been tempting people to take them off. But the Bible says women are to adorn themselves in modest apparel (1 Timothy 2:9), and there seems to be a direct correlation between spiritual maturity and modesty.

It takes moral courage to dress in an appropriate way, but that courage never escapes the notice of God. Plan your wardrobe today as you would plan your life, knowing that you have a loving Father to please.

XERXES

Clear Thinking

By the time the apostle Paul counseled Timothy to "use a little wine for your stomach's sake" (1 Timothy 5:23) King Xerxes had long since destroyed himself with too much "medicine."

NAME: "Prince" or "Chief" ???
DATE: 5th Century BC
IDENTIFICATION: King of Persia; husband of Esther; also called Ahasuerus
STORY LINE: Ahasuerus ruled vast empire; drunkenness destroyed him
READ IT IN THE BIBLE: Esther 1:1–2:17

Xerxes succeeded his father, Darius Hystaspis, in 485 BC. In the Bible we know him as Ahasuerus, the husband of Queen Esther. From the Book of Esther we gain some insight into just how powerful and rich this king was. His empire was vast, stretching from India to Ethiopia. It took one hundred eighty days to show his officials the extent of his net worth. He built the capital cities of Susa and Persepolis. Little wonder he was known as Xerxes the Great.

According to the Greek historian Herodotus, in the third year of his reign Xerxes held a convocation of his leaders to plan an invasion of Greece. The Book of Esther begins with a banquet scene that probably reflects that convocation. There Xerxes, in a drunken stupor, called for his first wife, Vashti, to display her beauty before his drunken friends. Vashti refused and Xerxes had her banished, replacing her with Esther.

The Bible says there is something better than wine for determining future plans. "Therefore do not be unwise, but understand what the will of the Lord is. And do not be drunk with wine, in which is dissipation; but be filled with the Spirit." (Ephesians 5:17–18).

Excess wine leads to unclear thinking (Proverbs 20:1). Being filled with God's Spirit leads to joyful thinking (Acts 13:52). Xerxes' rule ended in 465 BC when he was assassinated in his bedchamber by a courtier. Be filled with the Holy Spirit instead of wine, and you'll have a much brighter future.

ZACCHAEUS

The Wee Little Man

Richard Simkanin, saying the federal government is "in rebellion against the Republic of Texas," was convicted in January 2004 of twenty–nine counts of violating U.S. income tax laws. Simkanin's case may be a bit extreme, but no one likes paying taxes or tax collectors.

NAME: "Pure"

DATE: 1st Century AD

IDENTIFICATION: Chief tax collector of Jericho; hated by the people

STORY LINE: When Zacchaeus met Jesus, there was a dramatic change

READ IT IN THE BIBLE: Luke 19:1–10

The most famous tax collector in the Bible was a wee little man named Zacchaeus. As the head of the regional tax office at Jericho, he had grown wealthy by overcharging the people for their taxes, and they hated him for it.

One day Jesus passed through Jericho. Zacchaeus wanted to see Him, but Zacchaeus couldn't see over the crowd because of his stature. He was a sinner too short to see. Then he had a bright idea. He ran ahead of Jesus, climbed up into a sycamore tree, and suddenly became a sinner too high to hide. Jesus instructed Zacchaeus to come down because He wanted to be the guest at the tax collector's house.

So radically changed was Zacchaeus by meeting Jesus in a saving way that the little man became too convicted to continue in his sin. He vowed to make restitution fourfold to all those he had cheated, even though Levitical Law only required full restitution plus a twenty percent penalty (Leviticus 6:1–5).

Zacchaeus' conversion from charlatan to Christian was so dramatic that Jesus used it to teach us why He came to earth. "For the Son of Man has come to seek and to save that which was lost" (Luke 19:10). The wee little man demonstrates that we cannot hide from the Lord, but we can be found and saved by Him. Be glad today that Jesus is still seeking and saving the lost.

For the Son of Man has come to seek and to save that which was lost.

—Luke 19:10

ZECHARIAH

The Piercing of the Christ

When Mel Gibson's movie *The Passion of the Christ* was released, people lined up to see the graphic violence depicting Christ's crucifixion. For many, it was their first encounter with this torturous form of

NAME: "Jehovah Remembers"

DATE: 5th Century BC

IDENTIFICATION: Son of Berekiah; prophet in the days of Ezra

STORY LINE: Zechariah was perhaps the most messianic of prophets

READ IT IN THE BIBLE: Zechariah 2:1–13; 3:8; 6:1–13; 9:9; 12:10; 14:1–9

death, but it was not a surprise for those who have read John's crucifixion account.

John recorded, "But one of the soldiers pierced His side with a spear, and immediately blood and water came out" (John 19:34). John added that this was done in fulfillment of the prophetic statement, "They shall look on Him whom they pierced" (v. 37).

Long before *The Passion of the Christ,* Zechariah was

focusing on the life and death of the Messiah. A contemporary of the prophet Haggai, Zechariah was a leader in the restoration of Israel following their Babylonian Captivity. God used him to provide more prophetic information about Jesus Christ than any other prophet. The Book of Zechariah is the most Messianic of all the Old Testament books, containing eight specific references to the Messiah in its twelve chapters.

Perhaps the most remarkable of these references is Zechariah 12:10, which anticipates the response of the nation of Israel to Jesus as Savior and Messiah. One day the Jewish people will realize the significance of Jesus' death, and that will lead to their repentance and salvation (Romans 11:25–27). Nearly five hundred years before the passion of the Christ, and two thousand five hundred years before the film, Zechariah was describing the manner of Jesus' death to save us from our sins.

Don't allow this day to end without taking time to thank Jesus for His sacrifice at Calvary. Read John's passion story again, and look on Jesus who was pierced for you.

ZERUBBABEL

The Mark of the "Z"

When I was a boy one of my favorite heroes was Zorro, the legendary nobleman with black mask and flashing sword who eased the oppression of the *alcalde* on the peasants in old California. He came out of

NAME: "Offspring of Babylon"
DATE: 6th Century BC
IDENTIFICATION: Son of Shealtiel, he led the return to Jerusalem; built Second Temple
STORY LINE: Zerubbabel's work was not spectacular, not appreciated
READ IT IN THE BIBLE: Ezra 3:1–12; Haggai 2:1–23

nowhere and left behind only thankful people and the mark of the "Z."

The Bible has its own Zorro who came out of nowhere and left his mark on thankful people. His name also begins with a "Z"—Zerubbabel. Born the son of Shealtiel in Babylonian Captivity, he was the grandson of Jehoiachin, the captive king of Judah (1 Chronicles 3:17–19). That means Zerubbabel was a descendant of David and ancestor of Jesus. But in Babylon, his stature was diminished to captive. Diminished, that is, until Cyrus allowed the Jews to return to their homeland and rebuild their temple.

Suddenly the people needed a leader, a hero, someone who could leave the mark of the "Z", if you will. Zerubbabel rose to the challenge. He led the first group of captives back to Jerusalem and began rebuilding the temple on the site of Solomon's temple. When the work was finally finished, Zerubbabel's temple was dedicated with a great celebration that climaxed with the observance of the Passover (Ezra 6:19).

Zerubbabel came out of nowhere, but served tirelessly and faithfully. God had a special "well done" for Zerubbabel. He said, I will "make you like a signet ring, for I have chosen you" (Haggai 2:23). If you are living in "nowhere," be encouraged. God may call you out of nowhere to do more than you could ever dream. So be ready. It could happen today.

FOR MORE INFORMATION

Dr. Woodrow Kroll is president and senior Bible teacher for the international media ministry "Back to the Bible." The *Back to the Bible* radio broadcast, in one of twenty-five languages, can be heard by more than 50 percent of the world's population every day. Dr. Kroll is the author of more than three dozen books. His clear, incisive teaching of the Word keeps him in demand as a speaker all over the world. Says Woodrow Kroll, "My greatest joy is preaching the Word of God." He and his wife, Linda, reside in Ashland, Nebraska, near the international headquarters of Back to the Bible.

Here's how you can reach Back to the Bible:

00